LOVE DUET

AND OTHER
CURIOUS STORIES
ABOUT MUSIC

LOVE DUET

AND OTHER
CURIOUS STORIES
ABOUT MUSIC

Selected by

CHRISTOPHER
ONDAATJE

RARE BOOKS AND BERRY
2013

First published in 2013 by
Rare Books and Berry, High Street, Porlock, Minehead, Somerset TA24 8PU

Introduction © 2013 Christopher Ondaatje

'Love Duet' © 2013 Christopher Ondaatje

'The Alien Corn' by W. Somerset Maugham © United Agents on behalf of The
Literary Fund

'The Second Sense' by Nadine Gordimer © A.P. Watt at United Agents on behalf of
Nadine Gordimer

'Edward the Conqueror' by Roald Dahl © David Higham Literary Film and TV
Agents

'An Argument for Richard Strauss' and 'CODA: Glenn Gould in Conversation with
Tim Page' © Glenn Gould Limited

'Howards End' by E.M. Forster © The Provost and Scholars of King's College,
Cambridge and The Society of Authors as the E.M. Forster Estate

'Doctor Faustus' by Thomas Mann © Regal Literary, Inc. as agents for S. Fischer
Verlag

'Trio' © 2013 Rohan de Saram

A CIP catalogue record for this title is available from the British Library

ISBN 978-0-9563867-5-5

Designed and typeset in Garamond at Alacrity, Sandford, Somerset

Printed and bound by Henry Ling Ltd, Dorchester, Dorset

CONTENTS

LIST OF ILLUSTRATIONS

ACKNOWLEDGEMENTS

The publishers are grateful for permission to reprint the following pieces from previously published copyright material:

'The Alien Corn' by W. Somerset Maugham from *The Collected Stories of W. Somerset Maugham*, Penguin, reprinted by permission of United Agents on behalf of The Literary Fund.

'The Second Sense' by Nadine Gordimer from *Beethoven was One-Sixteenth Black and Other Stories*, Bloomsbury, 2008, reprinted by permission of A.P. Watt at United Agents on behalf of Nadine Gordimer.

'Edward the Conqueror' by Roald Dahl from *Kiss Kiss*, Penguin, reprinted by permission of David Higham Literary Film and TV Agents.

'An Argument for Richard Strauss' and 'CODA: Glenn Gould in Conversation with Tim Page' from *The Glenn Gould Reader*, edited by Tim Page, Alfred A. Knopf, 1989. Property of Glenn Gould Limited. Used by permission courtesy of the Glenn Gould Estate.

'Howards End' from *Howards End* by E.M. Forster, Penguin English Library, 2012, reprinted by permission of The Provost and Scholars of King's College, Cambridge and The Society of Authors as the E.M. Forster Estate.

"Doctor Faustus' from *Doctor Faustus: The Life of the German Composer Adrian Leverkühn as Told by a Friend* by Thomas Mann, S. Fischer Verlag, 1947, reprinted by permission of Regal Literary, Inc. as agents for S. Fischer Verlag. From Thomas Mann, *Doktor Faustus: Das Leben des deutschen Tonsetzers*, Adrian Leverkühn erzählt von einem Freunde, © 1947 by Fischer Verlag GmbH, Frankfurt am Main, all rights reserved by S. Fischer Verlag GmbH.

Non-copyright material has been taken from the following publications:

'A Wagner Matinée' by Willa Cather, a story from *Youth and The Bright Medusa*, Alfred A. Knopf, 1920.

'The Music on the Hill' by 'Saki' (H.H. Munro), a story from *The Chronicles of Clovis*, John Lane, The Bodley Head, 1926.

'The Kreutzer Sonata' by Leo Tolstóy, translated by Leo Wiener from the *Complete Works of Count Tolstóy*, Volume XVIII, Chapter 23, J.M. Dent & Co, 1904.

'Swann in Love' (an extract) by Marcel Proust, translated by C.K. Scott Moncrieff from *Swann's Way, Remembrance of Things Past*, Random House, 1934.

'Rothschild's Fiddle' by Anton Chekhov, translated by Marian Fell, a story from *Russian Silhouettes: More Stories of Russian Life*, Charles Scribner's Sons, 1915.

'An Opus II' by Robert Schumann, a recent translation from *Allgemeine Musikalische Zeitung*, December 7, 1831.

The publishers express their thanks to the following sources for permission to reproduce illustrated material. In the event that any omissions have occurred, proper acknowledgements will be made in future editions.

Page

12   Lebrecht
16   Leemage/Lebrecht Music & Arts
28   De Agostini/Lebrecht Music & Arts
33   DEA Picture Library/De Agostini Picture Library/Getty Images
38   De Agostini/Lebrecht Music & Arts
84   culture-images/Lebrecht
92   SuperStock/Getty Images
104 Henri Lehmann/The Bridgeman Art Library/Getty Images
117 Franz Seraph von Lenbach/The Bridgeman Art Library/Getty Images
128 culture-images/Lebrecht

131 Lebrecht Music & Arts
134 De Agostini Picture Library/Getty Images
140 culture-images/Lebrecht
147 FPG/Keystone/Getty Images
154 De Agostini/Lebrecht Music & Arts
161 Keystone/Hulton Archive/Getty Images
168 The Bridgeman Art Library/Getty Images
171 Imagno/Hulton Archive/Getty Images
174 Lebrecht Music & Arts
177 Imagno/Lebrecht
180 Lebrecht Music & Arts
194 Universal Images Group/Getty Images
197 SuperStock/Getty Images
200 John F. Ross/Lebrecht Music & Arts
205 De Agostini/Lebrecht Music & Arts
213 De Agostini/Lebrecht Music & Arts

Front cover: Les Deux Soeurs by Theodore Chasseriau (1819-1856), Musée du Louvre, Paris, Leemage/Lebrecht Music & Arts

Back cover: The Orchestra at the Opera House by Edgar Degas, (1834-1917), Mondadori Portfolio/UIG/Getty Images

Guido monachus   Theodaldus ep̄s.

F A B C D E F G a h b c d e f g d

INTRODUCTION

I MUST ADMIT that I was inspired to write "Love Duet" only after I met the two young musicians from Switzerland, Fiona and Ambra Albek, the Albek Duo. Apart from being totally absorbed by the twin sisters' performances, suddenly everything I had been taught at school simply seemed to flood back to me again. I have always been fascinated by music and believe it to be one of the great innovations of civilisation. Civilisation is after all a triumph of mind over matter, and reason over instinct.

It was Pope Gregory, in the 6th century, who first devised a method of writing down music, and Gregorian chants began to be organised into four, then eight and finally into twelve modes. These chants were developed mainly in Western and Central Europe during the 9th and 10th centuries, with later additions and redactions. The chant was traditionally sung by choirs of men and boys in churches, or else by women and men of religious orders in their chapels. In the 11th century the monk Guido of Arezzo invented a new form of music notation, introducing the notes *do, re, mi, fa, so, la* and *ti* which were drawn on a staff. These have been elaborated over time but the system we use today owes its invention to Guido. Later the madrigal, a form of secular vocal music for multiple voices, first appeared in Italy and became very popular during the Renaissance. The Italian composer Claudio Monteverdi wrote instrumental accompaniments for madrigals, and by adding dramatic elements he went on to compose the world's first operas.

By the late 1600s the Baroque era was emerging. Fashionably, composers were employed by royalty and the wealthy, and many

Guido d'Arezzo (or Gui Aretinus, 995-1050) with pupil Theodal (Teobaldo) playing a monochord. Guido, a Benedictine monk, was renowned for introducing the musical line system. Engraving from *Scriptires ecclesiastici de musica sacra* by Martin Gerbert (1720-1793), 1784.

were also employed by churches to write music for masses. This began to change the status of music because composers like Handel, Bach and Vivaldi were professionals who were paid to compose many of the works that are still well-known today. The classical period lasted well into the 1800s, yielding some of the most popular composers in history. Then the Romantic era emerged in the mid 1800s and saw the birth of emotional and poetic structure in music. Musicians like Chopin, Liszt and Brahms established their reputations at this time.

The Mecca for composers during the Romantic period was the Austrian capital, Vienna, home of the Strausses, which became the centre of classical music. Composers such as Tchaikovsky, Dvorak and Rachmaninoff created their work from their homes rather than from churches. This new music was sometimes based on local folk music, elaborated into compositions which remained extremely popular even in the 20th century. Later composers to emerge included Debussy, Stravinsky and Prokofiev.

I have selected in this book some of the musical stories and opinions that most affected me: Somerset Maugham's heart-rending "The Alien Corn" and Willa Cather's sensitive "A Wagner Matinée" have been included; as well as Anton Chekhov's "Rothschild's Fiddle" and an excerpt from Tolstoy's *The Kreutzer Sonata*. Two extraordinary stories from "Saki" (H.H. Munro) and Roald Dahl are here, as well as some cryptic comments and opinions from Glenn Gould which may change your interpretation of some composers' works as well as of him. An extract from Thomas Mann's *Doctor Faustus* on Beethoven's late piano sonatas – each a puzzlement and a joy – is included, and some vignettes from other literature including E.M. Forster's *Howards End*; and Proust muses on music in *Remembrance of Things Past*. Many of these authors' opinions have changed my attitude to music, and one cannot help but observe that personal relationships have often affected composers' works themselves as is the case of Schumann and Brahms. I have found that the more you know the more you get out of the performance. Putting this book together has been one of my most joyous learning experiences.

CHRISTOPHER ONDAATJE

LOVE DUET

Christopher Ondaatje

NOT LONG AGO I accompanied a friend who is a professional music critic to a concert at London's Wigmore Hall. He had mentioned that the Dorino Duo were going to perform there, and I had immediately agreed to go, because I have long admired them. In fact I wouldn't have missed the concert for the world, because to me no chamber duo can match the Dorino Duo for beauty of expression and depth of musicianship. Not only is their stage presence captivating and their ability to communicate the joy of music-making to their audience unrivalled, they also have an astonishing personal story, which I eventually got to hear from their very own lips. Of course, my critic friend knew only about their performances, nothing about their remarkable private life.

The first time I heard the Dorino Duo was about ten years ago in the Utzon Room of the Sydney Opera House, one of the world's most beautiful small performance spaces, overlooking the waters of Sydney Harbour, while I was in Sydney to give some lectures about my travels in the East. I still remember their unusual musical programme. They played a brief sonata by the Spanish composer Joaquín Turina that combined classical restraint with an intoxicating dash of Andalusia, then a short sonata by Mozart, then Bartók's Rumanian folk dances for viola and piano, and finally two arrangements by Alessandro Lucchetti based on Puccini's *Tosca* and *La Bohème*. Everything was performed with a delightful exuberance and panache, but the interpretations were never superficial or

17

exaggerated, always meticulous and expressive. The performance seemed to appeal to all of the audience's senses at once. Almost from the beginning, we were enchanted by the spontaneous freshness of the music and the eclectic choice of pieces. It was no wonder, I remember thinking, that the Duo had already enjoyed resounding acclaim in many parts of the world.

As an encore, they gave us two emotional pieces by the American composer William Perry, *Berliner Lied* for viola and piano, and *Broadway Ballet*, which form part of more than two hundred scores written by Perry for the New York Museum of Modern Art's silent film collection. Perry is a supreme melodist and the Duo had the gift of making just the right harmonic gestures at critical moments, lifting what was a wonderful tune from being something merely sentimental to the level of the intensely romantic. They seemed to have an uncanny ability to evoke bygone places and periods – Berlin and New York in the 1920s – with the most simple and direct of musical gestures. By the end of the concert, I freely admit that that I had fallen under their spell.

The Dorino Duo, Fiametta and Fiorenza, are twin sisters from Venice. Even if you didn't know this fact about them, it would be easy to guess it, not only from their similar looks but also from their evident intimacy: the special connection that is often seen in twins, like two peas in a pod. To me the sisters seemed to operate in perfect synchrony.

Their musical training reflects this relationship. Fiametta Dorino started to play the piano when she was seven. At the age of twelve, she attended the Swiss Italian Music Academy in Lugano, then the Musikhochschule in Zurich, and finally the well-known International Piano Academy in Imola, Italy, where she graduated with a Master's degree, playing as a duo with Fiorenza. Her favourite composers at this time were Chopin, Schumann, Brahms, Mozart and J.S. Bach. Fiorenza also started playing – violin and viola – when she was seven.

She too graduated at the Swiss Italian Music Academy before going to the Musikhochschule in Zurich and winning a Concert Diploma with top marks and a distinction. Then she graduated from the International Music Academy in Imola alongside Fiametta. Her chief inspirations were earlier violinists: Jascha Heifetz, Yehudi Menuhin and Ginette Neveu, the Frenchwoman who died so tragically young in an air crash in 1949.

However, the twin sisters didn't start playing together seriously until their twenty-first year. Soon after their debut in Italy as the Dorino Duo, they embarked on a youthful concert tour with grace, bravura and originality, which quickly led to an increasing demand for their performances around the world. It was at this time that I heard them play in Sydney.

Now, a decade later, there must have been at least five hundred people sitting in the Wigmore Hall, watching the two musicians on the familiar small raised stage beneath the hall's cupola and mural depicting the Soul of Music. The acoustics were superb, as always for chamber music at the Wigmore. Once again, I found myself enthralled.

The Duo's programme was, as usual, exceptionally varied. First came Manuel de Falla's *Suite Populaire Espagnole* for violin and piano, written in Paris by the Spanish composer in 1914, derived from his earlier *Canciones Populares Españolas* for voice and piano. Quite wonderfully, it preserved the melodies of the traditional Spanish songs, harmonizing them with piano accompaniments using natural overtones to accompany the notes of the melodies. Then came some film-related music, *Amarcord* by Nino Rota, a fantasy from Federico Fellini movies arranged by Lucchetti. Then Isaac Albéniz's *Hojas de Album Opus 165 "España"*, which was rather dry and quite brief but very typical of Albéniz's modal harmonies and his idiomatic suggestions of popular folk themes. After this there was a complete change: the Duo played Frank Bridge's rather sad *Allegro*

Appassionato and *Pensiero*, which I thought combined an extraordinary treatment of rhythm by Fiametta and a highly emotional performance by Fiorenza on her viola. Then, Bedřich Smetana's symphonic poems, *Má Vlast*. Finally, there was a reprise, at least for me, of Lucchetti's fantasy based on *La Bohème*. I have heard the versatile Lucchetti's compositions many times, but this arrangement, which had been written specially for the Dorino Duo, never fails to exert its magic. When it was over, I felt emotionally drained, hardly able to move, definitely not in the mood to go and congratulate the Duo, as I normally do after a performance.

My critic friend must have felt the same, because he didn't speak. We said nothing to each other for several minutes, as we watched the audience get up from their seats and gradually, in good order, file their way sideways to the corridors that led to the Wigmore Hall exits. And then, for some inexplicable reason, breaking the spell I remarked: "They have a secret, you know."

"What?" my friend asked. I didn't say anything.

"What secret?" he asked again.

"You know the twins quite well. You've chatted to them many times at parties after concerts," I said. "Surely you must have wondered how two such incredibly attractive and talented women could manage their busy working lives, constantly on tour under the spotlight, without apparently ever arguing or fighting or even having a serious difference of opinion."

"The thought has crossed my mind occasionally," he admitted. "But they seem so perfectly content and in tune with each other that I really didn't give it much thought."

"Well, you're right. And that's the way it was until about eight years ago when they were on a tour of Pakistan and India, and staying at the Taj Mahal Hotel overlooking Apollo Bunder in Mumbai, what used to be called Bombay. They had just finished their last concert in one of the halls at the National Centre for the

Performing Arts and were at the small reception party that usually follows such affairs, when they were both introduced to a man. In international academic circles, Rustom Irani is quite well known as an archaeologist interested in the ancient Indus Valley civilization. But in Mumbai he is best known as the head of a wealthy Parsee family with a love of the arts, especially western classical music. Over the years, like many Parsee families, the Iranis have sponsored many local scholars and artists, including composers. Irani was also a widower, eminently eligible, an attractive man with a light complexion, lean and athletic with an aquiline nose and chiselled features – what you might call an aristocratic look. Perhaps in his late forties. He and Fiametta hit it off immediately. But it was fairly obvious that Fiorenza, too, was equally taken with Rustom.

"Now remember, this was the end of the Duo's tour, their last concert in the subcontinent. So the three of them spent the greater part of the rest of the evening together. When the party finally broke up, they arranged to meet the following day for lunch at the Taj.

"You can imagine the guarded conversation between them in the hotel that night. Until now, they had had differences of opinion over music and concert schedules and that sort of thing – but never a difference over a man. Of course, both of them had had relationships with men, but these had never amounted to much. Their lives had been far too busy. Now, very suddenly, when they were both heading for musical fame, each had met a man to whom she was seriously attracted, and a competition was inevitable. Although nothing was said that evening, both knew that such a rivalry could erupt and disrupt their partnership, and even possibly threaten their musical careers.

"They lunched in the Souk Restaurant on the top floor of the Taj, at one of the most romantic tables, next to windows from which they could see not only the nearby Gateway of India but also the outline of Elephanta Island and even the distant Nhava Sheva port. In fact, the air was so clear that a good part of south Mumbai was visible, including Malabar Hill on the far side of the Back Bay. To make matters worse, the elegant and charming Mr Irani seemed to be as keen on Fiorenza as he was on Fiametta. Both twins vied for his attention and he, as openly, encouraged their affections. It was a double *coup de foudre*, if such a thing exists. And not one of the triangle knew what to do next. Two days later, the twins were scheduled to fly back to Milan. They agreed to meet Rustom Irani again later that evening – this time at his mansion on Malabar Hill. 'My driver will pick you up at your hotel at seven o'clock,' he said. 'Dress casually, because I have a surprise for you.'

"The Parsees are Zoroastrians in religion, followers of the ancient Persian prophet, Zoroaster or Zarathustra. Their name, Parsee, was given to them after they emigrated from Persia following its conquest by the Arabs in the early eighth century. They moved to the western coast of India, first to Gujarat, later further south, where they eventually helped the British to build Bombay and settled in houses and mansions on Malabar Hill in the nineteenth century. A Parsee built the Taj Mahal Hotel. Nowadays, their mansions have a some-what faded grandeur, but more than enough to enchant the first-time visitor.

"When Fiametta and Fiorenza's suitor, Rustom Irani, greeted them at the doors of his mansion, he was dressed in traditional Parsee costume: shirt, pyjamas, long gown and turban. His shirt, or *sadara*, which is normally considered to be the most sacred garment because it is worn next to the skin, was like a vest made of fine but plain white linen. His black gown, extending down to his knees, was held around his waist with a *kusti*, or sacred cord, which was wrapped round three times and fastened in front with a double knot. His pyjamas were of red silk, fastened about his waist with a silken cord. His maroon-coloured turban was made of stiff material, quite like a

European hat but without any rim, and worn at an angle from the top of the forehead backwards. His shoes were of red morocco, turned up at the toes.

"Rustom warmly welcomed the excited girls. 'Now,' he said, 'for the surprise I promised you at lunchtime. If you are to enjoy my hospitality this evening, you must dress as ladies of this house. It will amuse you, and you will be much more comfortable.' Two female servants in waiting silently appeared and escorted Fiametta and Fiorenza to the private quarters. Here they shed their western clothes and were slipped into satin pyjamas, selected by them from a variety of textures and colours on offer that far excelled those worn by their host. Then they were enfolded in a maze of mysteriously wrapped silk. Many yards of silk were wound round their nether limbs, virtually concealing their bodies except for part of the bosom, and then thrown over their shoulders and heads, to droop on their left arms, as a shield against the gaze of any inquisitive stranger. After being draped with gold anklets, necklaces and earrings, the twins appeared to be more like houris, Persian ladies of paradise, in their ethereal balloons of silk, than earthly women. It was an utterly exotic experience, and the twins felt as if their world of make-believe was a wonderland. The dress of the Parsee ladies is renowned for its gorgeousness, and Fiametta and Fiorenza made a grand entrance as they were conducted out to meet their host.

"Despite their exoticism, Parsees are well known for having adjusted and adapted to the ways of their adopted land, mingling with other people and respecting their customs and ways of life while maintaining their own identity and remaining faithful to their own religion and customs. Rustom Irani was determined to live up to this reputation by entertaining his guests in as splendidly Parsee fashion as he could while also ensuring that they were comfortable and always at ease. He made himself into the perfect host. Parsee food is a mix of spices, dried fruits, nuts, eggs, chutneys and coconut.

Sauces, made from pomegranate, tamarind and lime are both sharp and rich at the same time, influenced by the Gujerati relish for sweet and sour. At any Parsee dinner, the succession of dishes is enough to halt outsiders in their tracks. Fiametta and Fiorenza, as they ate while listening to their host talking about the fascinating history of the Parsees, and telling him in turn about their lives as musicians, couldn't help wondering how he had managed to remain so athletic.

"Shortly before midnight, after a lull in the conversation, Rustom opened his heart to the twins. 'All the wonderful clothes and things you are wearing are a present to you from me. You look marvellous in them and you do not have to be at all ashamed of being seen in public in your finery. It suits you. But soon my driver will have to return you to your hotel. However, before he does, there is something important that I want to say. We have had a marvellous evening. In fact I cannot think when I have enjoyed myself more. You can see that I am more than attracted to both of you, and I feel sure that my feelings are reciprocated. If I were to feel the same way tomorrow as I do now, I would definitely ask one of you to marry me and to stay here with me in Mumbai. But that is an extremely difficult decision for me to make. And probably much harder for you. How can I possibly choose one of you? I can hardly tell you apart as it is. You are both incredibly beautiful, sensitive, and full of all the yearning and understanding that I so need in my life. It's now six years since my wife died of cancer, and I haven't forgotten the sadness, but I would like to remarry. More than that, it is important for my family that I have an heir, not only to inherit my fortune but to carry on my family responsibilities and family business. Are either of you prepared to leave the other and give up your musical career to marry me and live the life of a Parsee princess in what must seem to you to be a strange eastern country?'

"Coming as it did late in the evening, after such an intimate tête-à-tête, the question was certainly quite a shock. The twins had worked almost without pause to gain acceptance and acclaim in the musical world, and now they were faced with an awful dilemma. They were both stunned and silent.

"Then Fiametta, who was actually the elder twin by a few minutes, looked at Fiorenza and suggested, 'Why don't we meet tomorrow morning at ten o'clock and we'll give you our answer? It's much more than an important decision for us – it will change our entire lives. We are booked to catch the plane to Milan early the following morning. But if we come to the right decision, it won't matter that we shall be flying away, because our feelings will not change and we shall need time to adjust our lives accordingly. Our feelings for each other are as important now as our feelings for you and we must somehow sort out our confusion. Don't forget we have lived virtually all of our lives together, doing everything together and often making the same decisions at the same time – often without even consulting each other.'

"And there they left it. Fiametta and Fiorenza bid warm goodbyes and were driven back to their suite at the hotel, where they talked well into the night. The discussion was confused, tearful and often tender – but never angry. In the early hours, Fiametta, after a thoughtful silence said: 'I really want to marry Rustom. I love him, and I want to bear his children. Tell me truthfully – do you?'

"Fiorenza pondered, and said at long last, with tears in her eyes, 'I love Rustom too. But I'm not sure I want to give up everything I have, and I'm not sure I want all the responsibilities of a marriage and bringing up his children – particularly here in India. And I'm equally certain that I don't want to give up our musical career after everything we've worked so hard for and achieved. I can't imagine a life without you. I suppose I wouldn't even mind being Rustom's mistress – without any of the other responsibilities that you are so eager to assume. I would even like it. But how could this possibly happen? And how could you possibly agree to share your husband

25

with me? If there was any way we could do this, we could then keep our musical careers, have the man we both love, and still have each other. I promise never to make any undue demands on him or interfere with your marriage. This way neither of us would really be giving up anything, least of all our love for each other.'

"And that was how the long and extraordinary day finally ended. The exhausted twins went to sleep. They woke next morning feeling surprisingly refreshed, and both of them shared an unexpected and unfamiliar excitement. They hugged each other for a long while. Then Fiametta, again taking the lead, said: 'Don't say a word. Nothing at all. Let things happen as they will. Let's see what Rustom says when we meet him this morning. After all, I'm sure the decision is much harder for him than for us. Who knows, maybe he will come up with the answer and sort the whole thing out for us.'"

* * *

I stopped speaking. My companion and I were sitting practically alone in the empty Wigmore Hall, with the magic of the evening's music beginning to wear off. It was time to leave. Later, over a quick dinner, I explained that Fiametta did eventually marry Rustom Irani, and the twins do still live together – well, not quite – in the same compound on Malabar Hill. Fiametta has two young children, a boy Cyrus and a girl Baegan, with a beautiful oval face like her mother. The sisters still have their musical schedule, marginally less busy than before, playing concerts in Italy, Russia, China, England, Australia, France and of course India, where they help the philanthropic work of the Irani family's foundation. In fact, the Dorino Duo are extremely well known and in much demand all over the world. So far as I can tell when I meet them – which is somewhat less often, now that they live in India – they have a happy existence. As for the rest of us, we are lucky not to have lost one of the most talented musical duos in musical history but for the imaginative creativity and unselfishness of the younger of the two sisters. Sometimes the world works its wonders in strange ways, and sometimes insoluble problems are solved with secret innovative genius.

A WAGNER MATINÉE

Willa Cather

I RECEIVED ONE MORNING a letter, written in pale ink on glassy, blue-lined note-paper, and bearing the postmark of a little Nebraska village. This communication, worn and rubbed, looked as if it had been carried for some days in a coat pocket that was none too clean, was from my uncle Howard, and informed me that his wife had been left a small legacy by a bachelor relative, and that it would be necessary for her to go to Boston to attend to the settling of the estate. He requested me to meet her at the station and render her whatever services might be necessary. On examining the date indicated as that of her arrival, I found it to be no later than tomorrow. He had characteristically delayed writing until, had I been away from home for a day, I must have missed my aunt altogether.

The name of my Aunt Georgiana opened before me a gulf of recollection so wide and deep that, as the letter dropped from my hand, I felt suddenly as a stranger to all the present conditions of my existence, wholly ill at ease and out of place amid the familiar surroundings of my study. I became, in short, the gangling farmer-boy my aunt had known, scourged with chilblains and bashfulness, my hands cracked and sore from the corn husking. I sat again before her parlour organ, fumbling the scales with my stiff, red fingers, while she, beside me, made canvas mittens for the huskers.

The next morning, after preparing my landlady for a visitor, I set out for the station. When the train arrived I had some difficulty in finding my aunt. She was the last of the passengers to alight, and it

Portrait of Wilhelm Richard Wagner (Leipzig, 1813-Venice, 1883), German composer, librettist, conductor and essayst, by Franz von Lenbach (1836-1904), 1882.

was not until I got her into the carriage that she seemed really to recognize me. She had come all the way in a day coach; her linen duster had become black with soot and her black bonnet grey with dust during the journey. When we arrived at my boarding-house the landlady put her to bed at once and I did not see her again until the next morning.

Whatever shock Mrs. Springer experienced at my aunt's appearance, she considerably concealed. As for myself, I saw my aunt's battered figure with that feeling of awe and respect with which we behold explorers who have left their ears and fingers north of Franz-Joseph-Land, or their health somewhere along the Upper Congo. My Aunt Georgiana had been a music teacher at the Boston Conservatory, somewhere back in the latter sixties. One summer, while visiting in the little village among the Green Mountains where her ancestors had dwelt for generations, she had kindled the callow fancy of my uncle, Howard Carpenter, then an idle, shiftless boy of twenty-one. When she returned to her duties in Boston, Howard followed her, and the upshot of this infatuation was that she eloped with him to the Nebraska frontier. Carpenter, who, of course, had no money, took up a homestead in Red Willow County, fifty miles from the railroad. There they had measured off their land themselves, driving across the prairie in a wagon, to the wheel of which they had tied a red cotton handkerchief, and counting its revolutions. They built a dug-out in the red hillside, one of those cave dwellings whose inmates so often reverted to primitive conditions. Their water they got from the lagoons where the buffalo drank, and their slender stock of provisions was always at the mercy of bands of roving Indians. For thirty years my aunt had not been farther than fifty miles from the homestead.

I owed this woman most of the good that ever came my way in my boyhood, and had a reverential affection for her. During the years when I was riding herd for my uncle, my aunt, after cooking the three meals – the first of which was ready at six o'clock in the morning – and putting the six children to bed, would often stand until midnight at her ironing board, with me at the kitchen table beside her, hearing me recite Latin declensions and conjugations, gently shaking me when my drowsy head sank down over a page of irregular verbs. It was to her, at her ironing and mending, that I read my first Shakespeare, and her old text-book on mythology was the first that ever came into my empty hands. She taught me my scales and exercises on the little parlour organ which her husband had bought her after fifteen years during which she had not so much as seen a musical instrument. She would sit beside me by the hour, darning and counting, while I struggled with the "Joyous Farmer." She seldom talked to me about music, and I understood why. Once when I had been doggedly beating out some easy passages from an old score of *Euryanthe* I had found among her music books, she came up to me and, putting her hands gently over my eyes, gently drew my head back upon her shoulder, saying tremulously, "Don't love it so well, Clark, or it may be taken from you."

When my aunt appeared on the morning after her arrival in Boston, she was still in a semi-somnambulant state. She seemed not to realize that she was in the city where she had spent her youth, the place longed for hungrily half a lifetime. She had been so wretchedly train-sick throughout the journey that she had no recollection of anything but her discomfort, and, to all intents and purposes, there were but a few hours of nightmare between the farm in Red Willow County and my study on Newbury Street. I had planned a little pleasure for her that afternoon, to repay her for some of the glorious moments she had given me when we used to milk together in the straw-thatched cowshed and she, because I was more than usually tired, or because her husband had spoken sharply to me, would tell me of the splendid performance of the *Huguenots* she had seen in Paris, in her youth.

31

At two o'clock the Symphony Orchestra was to give a Wagner program, and I intended to take my aunt; though, as I conversed with her, I grew doubtful about her enjoyment of it. I suggested our visiting the Conservatory and the Common before lunch, but she seemed altogether too timid to wish to venture out. She questioned me absently about various changes in the city, but she was chiefly concerned that she had forgotten to leave instructions about feeding half-skimmed milk to a certain weakling calf, "old Maggie's calf, you know, Clark," she explained, evidently having forgotten how long I had been away. She was further troubled because she had neglected to tell her daughter about the freshly-opened kit of mackerel in the cellar, which would spoil if it were not used directly.

I asked her whether she had ever heard any of the Wagnerian operas, and found that she had not, though she was perfectly familiar with their respective situations, and had once possessed the piano score of *The Flying Dutchman*. I began to think it would be best to get her back to Red Willow County without waking her, and regretted having suggested the concert.

From the time we entered the concert hall, however, she was a trifle less passive and inert, and for the first time seemed to perceive her surroundings. I had felt some trepidation lest she might become aware of her queer, country clothes, or might experience some painful embarrassment at stepping suddenly into the world to which she had been dead for a quarter of a century. But, again, I found how superficially I had judged her. She sat looking about her with eyes as impersonal, almost as stony, as those with which the granite Rameses in a museum watched the froth and fret that ebbs and flows about his pedestal. I have seen this same aloofness in old miners who drift into the Brown hotel at Denver, their pockets full of bullion, their linen soiled, their haggard faces unshaven; standing in the thronged corridors as solitary as though they were still in a frozen camp on the Yukon.

Ludwig II of Bavaria and Richard Wagner in Hohenschwangau.

The matinée audience was made up chiefly of women. One lost the contour of faces and figures, indeed any effect of line whatever, and there was only the colour of bodices past counting, the shimmer of fabrics soft and firm, silky and sheer; red, mauve, pink, blue, lilac, purple, écru, rose, yellow, cream and white, all the colours that an impressionist finds in a sunlit landscape, with here and there the dead shadow of a frock coat. My Aunt Georgiana regarded them as though they had been so many daubs of tube paint on a palette.

When the musicians came out and took their places, she gave a little stir of anticipation, and looked with quickening interest down over the rail at the invariable grouping, perhaps the first wholly familiar thing that had greeted her eye since she had left old Maggie and her weakling calf. I could feel how all those details sank into her soul, for I had not forgotten how they had sunk into mine when I came fresh from ploughing forever and forever between green aisles of corn, where, as in a treadmill, one might walk from daybreak to dusk without perceiving a shadow of change. The clean profiles of the musicians, the gloss of their linen, the dull black of their coats, the beloved shapes of the instruments, the patches of yellow light on the smooth, varnished bellies of the 'cellos and the bass viols in the rear, the restless, wind-tossed forest of fiddle necks and bows – I recalled how, in the first orchestra I ever heard, those long bow-strokes seemed to draw the heart out of me, as a conjurer's stick reels out yards of paper ribbon from a hat.

The first number was the *Tannhauser* overture. When the horns drew out the first strain of the Pilgrim's chorus, Aunt Georgiana clutched my coat sleeve. Then it was I first realized that for her this broke a silence of thirty years. With the battle between the two motives, with the frenzy of the Venusberg theme and its ripping of strings, there came to me an overwhelming sense of the waste and wear we are so powerless to combat; and I saw again the tall, naked house of the prairie, black and grim as a wooden fortress; the black pond where I had learned to swim, its margin pitted with sun-dried cattle tracks; the rain gullied clay banks about the naked house, the four dwarf ash seedlings where the dish-cloths were always hung to dry before the kitchen door. The world there was the flat world of the ancients; to the east, a cornfield that stretched to daybreak; to the west, a corral that reached to sunset; between, the conquests of peace, dearer-bought than those of war.

The overture closed, my aunt released my coat sleeve, but she said nothing. She sat staring dully at the orchestra. What, I wondered, did she get from it? She had been a good pianist in her day, I knew, and her musical education had been broader than that of most music teachers of a quarter of a century ago. She had often told me of Mozart's operas and Meyerbeer's and I could remember hearing her sing, years ago, certain melodies of Verdi. When I had fallen ill with a fever in her house she used to sit by my cot in the evening – when the cool, night wind blew in through the faded mosquito netting tacked over the window and I lay watching a certain bright star that burned red over the cornfield – and sing "Home to our mountains, O, let us return!" in a way fit to break the heart of a Vermont boy near dead of homesickness already.

I watched her closely through the prelude to *Tristan and Isolde*, trying vainly to conjecture what that seething turmoil of strings and winds might mean to her, but she sat mutely staring at the violin bows that drove obliquely downward, like the pelting streaks of rain in a summer shower. Had this music any message for her? Had she enough left to at all comprehend this power which had kindled the world since she had left it? I was in a fever of curiosity, but Aunt Georgiana sat silent upon her peak in Darien. She preserved this utter immobility throughout the number from *The Flying Dutchman*, though her fingers worked mechanically upon her black dress, as if, of themselves, they were recalling the piano score they had once played. Poor hands! They had been stretched and twisted into mere tentacles to hold and lift and knead with; – on one of them a thin, worn band that had once been a wedding ring. As I pressed and gently quieted one of those groping hands, I remembered with quivering eyelids their services for me in other days.

Soon after the tenor began the "Prize Song," I heard a quick drawn breath and turned to my aunt. Her eyes were closed, but the tears were glistening on her cheeks, and I think, in a moment more, they were in my eyes as well. It never really died, then – the soul which can suffer so excruciatingly and so interminably; it withers to the outward eye only; like that strange moss which can lie on a dusty shelf half a century and yet, if placed in water, grows green again. She wept so throughout the development and elaboration of the melody.

During the intermission before the second half, I questioned my aunt and found that the "Prize Song" was not new to her. Some years before there had drifted to the farm in Red Willow County a young German, a tramp cow-puncher, who had sung in the chorus at Bayreuth when he was a boy, along with other peasant boys and girls. Of a Sunday morning he used to sit on his gingham-sheeted bed in the hands' bedroom which opened off the kitchen, cleaning the leather of his boots and saddle, singing the "Prize Song," while my aunt went about her work in the kitchen. She had hovered over him until she had prevailed upon him to join the country church, though his sole fitness for this step, in so far as I could gather, lay in his boyish face and his possession of this divine melody. Shortly afterward, he had gone to town on the Fourth of July, been drunk for several days, lost his money at a faro table, ridden a saddled Texas steer on a bet, and disappeared with a fractured collar-bone. All this my aunt told me huskily, wonderingly, as though she were talking in the weak lapses of illness.

"Well, we have come to better things than the old *Trovatore* at any rate, Aunt Georgie?" I queried, with a well meant effort at jocularity.

Her lip quivered and she hastily put her handkerchief up to her mouth. From behind it she murmured, "And you have been hearing this ever since you left me, Clark?" Her question was the gentlest and saddest of reproaches.

The second half of the program consisted of four numbers from the *Ring*, and closed with Siegfried's funeral march. My aunt wept quietly, but almost continuously, as a shallow vessel overflows in a rain-storm. From time to time her dim eyes looked up at the lights, burning softly under their dull glass globes.

The deluge of sound poured on and on; I never knew what she found in the shining current of it; I never knew how far it bore her, or past what happy islands. From the trembling of her face I could well believe that before the last number she had been carried out where the myriad graves are, into the grey, nameless burying grounds of the sea; or into some world of death vaster yet, where, from the beginning of the world, hope has lain down with hope and dream with dream and, renouncing, slept.

The concert was over; the people filed out of the hall chattering and laughing, glad to relax and find the living level again, but my kinswoman made no effort to rise. The harpist slipped the green felt cover over his instrument; the flute-players shook the water from their mouthpieces; the men of the orchestra went out one by one, leaving the stage to the chairs and music stands, empty as a winter cornfield.

I spoke to my aunt. She burst into tears and sobbed pleadingly. "I don't want to go, Clark, I don't want to go!"

I understood. For her, just outside the concert hall, lay the black pond with the cattle-tracked bluffs; the tall, unpainted house, with weather-curled boards, naked as a tower; the crook-backed ash seedlings where the dish-cloths hung to dry, the gaunt, moulting turkeys picking up refuse about the kitchen door.

37

THE ALIEN CORN

W. Somerset Maugham

Somerset Maugham's controversial masterpiece 'The Alien Corn', written in 1931, has sometimes been considered anti-Semitic. It is not. Maugham is not critical of religious and cultural differences; he writes instead about the vocation of the artist and the power of money, and how the artist must rely on it to make his art possible and acceptable. This sensitive story is about a Jewish family's assimilation into the English aristocracy and its shock when their oldest son rejects the trappings of nobility to try to become a concert pianist. It is a study of cultural alienation and the striving to belong, a story of immigrants in an alien country. The life of the tragic hero shows that belonging is perhaps the only way to recapture one's own heritage.

I HAD KNOWN the Blands a long time before I discovered that they had any connexion with Ferdy Rabenstein. Ferdy must have been nearly fifty when I first knew him and at the time of which I write he was well over seventy. He had altered little. His hair, coarse but abundant and curly, was white, but he had kept his figure and held himself as gallantly as ever. It was not hard to believe that in youth he had been as beautiful as people said. He had still his fine Semitic profile and the lustrous black eyes that had caused havoc in so many a Gentile breast. He was very tall, lean, with an oval face and a clear skin. He wore his clothes very well and in evening dress, even now, he was one of the handsomest men I had ever seen. He wore then large black pearls in his shirt-front and platinum and sapphire rings on his fingers. Perhaps he was rather flashy, but you felt it was so

39

Portrait of a Musician by Leonardo da Vinci (1452-1519). Tempera and oil on panel, 40 x 30cm, c.1490.

much in character that it would have ill become him to be anything else.

'After all, I am an Oriental,' he said. 'I can carry a certain amount of barbaric magnificence.'

I have often thought that Ferdy Rabenstein would make an admirable subject for a biography. He was not a great man, but within the limits he set himself he made of his life a work of art. It was a masterpiece in little, like a Persian miniature, and derived its interest from its perfection. Unfortunately the materials are scanty. They would consist of letters that may very well have been destroyed and the recollections of people who are old now and will soon be dead. His memory is extraordinary, but he would never write his memoirs, for he looks upon his past as a source of purely private entertainment; and he is a man of the most perfect discretion. Nor do I know anyone who could do justice to the subject but Max Beerbohm. There is no one else in this hard world of today who can look upon the trivial with such tender sympathy and wring such a delicate pathos from futility. I wonder that Max, who must have known Ferdy much better than I, and long before, was never tempted to exercise his exquisite fancy on such a theme. He was born for Max to write about. And who should have illustrated the elegant book that I see in my mind's eye but Aubrey Beardsley! Thus would have been erected a monument of triple brass and the ephemera imprisoned to succeeding ages in the amber's translucency.

Ferdy's conquests were social and his venue was the great world. He was born in South Africa and did not come to England till he was twenty. For some time he was on the Stock Exchange, but on the death of his father he inherited a considerable fortune, and retiring from business devoted himself to the life of a man about town. At that period English society was still a closed body and it was not easy for a Jew to force its barriers, but to Ferdy they fell like the walls of Jericho. He was handsome, he was rich, he was a sportsman and he was good company. He had a house in Curzon Street, furnished with the most beautiful French furniture, and a French chef, and a brougham. It would be interesting to know the first steps in his wonderful career: they are lost in the dark abysm of time. When I first met him he had been long established as one of the smartest men in London: this was at a very grand house in Norfolk to which I had been asked as a promising young novelist by the hostess who took an interest in letters, but the company was very distinguished and I was over-awed. We were sixteen, and I felt shy and alone among these Cabinet Ministers, great ladies, and peers of the realm who talked of people and things of which I knew nothing. They were civil to me, but indifferent, and I was conscious that I was something of a burden to my hostess. Ferdy saved me. He sat with me, walked with me, and talked with me. He discovered that I was a writer and we discussed the drama and the novel: he learnt that I had lived much on the Continent and he talked to me pleasantly of France, Germany and Spain. He seemed ready to seek my society. He gave me the flattering impression that he and I stood apart from the other members of the company and by our conversation upon affairs of the spirit made that of the rest of them, the political situation, the scandal of somebody's divorce, and the growing disinclination of pheasants to be killed, seem a little ridiculous. But if Ferdy had at the bottom of his heart a feeling of ever so faint a contempt for the hearty British gentry that surrounded us I am sure that it was only to me that he allowed an inkling of it to appear, and looking back I cannot but wonder whether it was not after all a suave and very delicate compliment that he paid me. I think of course that he liked to exercise his charm and I dare say the obvious pleasure his conversation gave me gratified him, but he could have had no motive for taking so much trouble over an obscure novelist other than his real interest in art and letters. I felt that he and I at bottom were equally alien in that company, I because I was a writer and he because he was a Jew, but

I envied the ease with which he bore himself. He was completely at home. Everyone called him Ferdy. He seemed to be always in good spirits. He was never at a loss for a quip, a jest, or a repartee. They liked him in that house because he made them laugh, but never made them uncomfortable by talking over their heads. He brought a faint savour of Oriental romance into their lives, but so cleverly that they only felt more English. You could never be dull when he was by and with him present you were safe from the fear of devastating silences that sometimes overwhelm a British company. A pause looked inevitable and Ferdy Rabenstein had broken into a topic that interested everyone. An invaluable asset to any party. He had an inexhaustible fund of Jewish stories. He was a very good mimic and he assumed the Yiddish accent and reproduced the Jewish gestures to perfection; his head sank into his body, his face grew cunning, his voice oily, and he was a rabbi or an old clothes merchant or a smart commercial traveller or a fat procuress in Frankfort. It was as good as a play. Because he was himself a Jew and insisted on it you laughed without reserve, but for my own part not without an under-current of discomfort. I was not quite sure of a sense of humour that made such cruel fun of his own race. I discovered afterwards that Jewish stories were his speciality and I seldom met him anywhere without hearing him tell sooner or later the last he had heard.

But the best story he told me on this occasion was not a Jewish one. It struck me so that I have never forgotten it, but for one reason or another I have never had occasion to tell it again. I give it here because it is a curious little incident concerning persons whose names at least will live in the social history of the Victorian Era and I think it would be a pity if it were lost. He told me then that once when quite a young man he was staying in the country in a house where Mrs Langtry, at that time at the height of her beauty and astounding reputation, was also a guest. It happened to be within driving distance of that in which lived the Duchess of Somerset, who had been Queen of Beauty at the Eglinton Tournament, and knowing her slightly, it occurred to him that it would be interesting to bring the two women together. He suggested it to Mrs Langtry, who was willing and forthwith wrote to the Duchess asking if he might bring the celebrated beauty to call on her. It was fitting, he said, that the loveliest woman of this generation (this was in the eighties) should pay her respects to the loveliest woman of the last. 'Bring her by all means,' answered the Duchess, 'but I warn you that it will be a shock to her.' They drove over in a carriage and pair, Mrs Langtry in a close-fitting blue bonnet with long satin strings, which showed the fine shape of her head and made her blue eyes even bluer, and were received by a little ugly old hag who looked with irony out of her beady eyes at the radiant beauty who had come to see her. They had tea, they talked, and they drove home again. Mrs Langtry was very silent and when Ferdy looked at her he saw that she was quietly weeping. When they got back to the house she went to her room and would not come down to dinner that night. For the first time she had realized that beauty dies.

Ferdy asked me for my address and a few days after I got back to London invited me to dinner. There were only six of us, an American woman married to an English peer, a Swedish painter, an actress, and a well-known critic. We ate very good food and drank excellent wine. The conversation was easy and intelligent. After dinner Ferdy was persuaded to play the piano. He only played Viennese waltzes, I discovered later that they were his speciality, and the light, tuneful, and sensual music seemed to accord well with his discreet flamboyance. He played without affectation, with a lilt, and he had a graceful touch. This was the first of a good many dinners I had with him, he would ask me two or three times a year, and as time passed I met him more and more frequently at other people's houses. I rose in the world and perhaps he came down a little. Of late years I had sometimes found him at parties where other Jews were and I fancied that I read in his

43

shining liquid eyes, resting for a moment on these members of his race, a certain good-natured amusement at the thought of what the world was coming to. There were people who said he was a snob, but I do not think he was; it just happened that in his early days he had never met any but the great. He had a real passion for art and in his commerce with those that produced it was at his best. With them he had never that faint air of persiflage which when he was with very grand persons made you suspect that he was never quite the dupe of their grandeur. His taste was perfect and many of his friends were glad to avail themselves of his knowledge. He was one of the first to value old furniture and he rescued many a priceless piece from the attics of ancestral mansions and gave it an honourable place in the drawing-room. It amused him to saunter round the auction rooms and he was always willing to give his advice to great ladies who desired at once to acquire a beautiful thing and make a profitable investment. He was rich and good-natured. He liked to patronize the arts and would take a great deal of trouble to get commissions for some young painter whose talent he admired or an engagement to play at a rich man's house for a violinist who could in no other way get a hearing. But he never let his rich man down. His taste was too good to deceive and civil though he might be to the mediocre he would not lift a finger to help them. His own musical parties, very small and carefully chosen, were a treat.

He never married.

'I am a man of the world,' he said, 'and I flatter myself that I have no prejudices, *tous les gouts sont dans la nature,* but I do not think I could bring myself to marry a Gentile. There's no harm in going to the opera in a dinner jacket, but it just would never occur to me to do so.'

'Then why didn't you marry a Jewess?'

(I did not hear this conversation, but the lively and audacious creature who thus tackled him told me of it.)

'Oh, my dear, our women are so prolific. I could not bear the thought of peopling the world with a little Ikey and a little Jacob and a little Rebecca and a little Leah and a little Rachel.'

But he had had affairs of note and the glamour of past romance still clung to him. He was in his youth of an amorous complexion. I have met old ladies who told me that he was irresistible, and when in reminiscent mood they talked to me of this woman and that who had completely lost her head over him, I divined that, such was his beauty, they could not find it in their hearts to blame them. It was interesting to hear of great ladies that I had read of in the memoirs of the day or had met as respectable dowagers garrulous over their grandsons at Eton or making a mess of a hand at bridge and bethink myself that they had been consumed with sinful passion for the handsome Jew. Ferdy's most notorious amour was with the Duchess of Hereford, the loveliest, the most gallant and dashing of the beauties at the end of Queen Victoria's reign. It lasted for twenty years. He had doubtless flirtations meanwhile, but their relations were stable and recognized. It was proof of his marvellous tact that when at last they ended he exchanged an ageing mistress for a loyal friend. I remember meeting the pair not so very long ago at luncheon. She was an old woman, tall and of a commanding presence, but with a mask of paint on a ravaged face. We were lunching at the Carlton and Ferdy, our host, came a few minutes late. He offered us a cocktail and the Duchess told him we had already had one.

'Ah, I wondered why your eyes were so doubly bright,' he said.

The old raddled woman flushed with pleasure.

My youth passed, I grew middle-aged, I wondered how soon I must begin to describe myself as elderly; I wrote books and plays, I travelled, I underwent experiences, I fell in love and out of it; and still I kept meeting Ferdy at parties. War broke out and was waged, millions of men were killed, and the face of the world was changed.

Ferdy did not like the war. He was too old to take part in it, and his German name was awkward, but he was discreet and took care not to expose himself to humiliation. His old friends were faithful to him and he lived in a dignified but not too strict seclusion. But then peace came and with courage he set himself to making the best of changed conditions. Society was mixed now, parties were rowdy, but Ferdy fitted himself to the new life. He still told his funny Jewish stories, he still played charmingly the waltzes of Strauss, he still went round auction rooms and told the new rich what they ought to buy. I went to live abroad, but whenever I was in London I saw Ferdy and now there was something a little uncanny in him. He did not give in. He had never known a day's illness. He seemed never to grow tired. He still dressed beautifully. He was interested in everybody. His mind was alert and people asked him to dinner, not for old times' sake, but because he was worth his salt. He still gave charming little concerts at his house in Curzon Street.

It was when he invited me to one of these that I made the discovery that started the recollections of him I have here set down. We were dining at a house in Hill Street, a large party, and the women having gone upstairs Ferdy and I found ourselves side by side. He told me that Lea Makart was coming to play for him on the following Friday evening and he would be glad if I would come.

'I'm awfully sorry,' I said, 'but I'm going down to the Blands.'

'What Blands?'

'They live in Sussex at a place called Tilby.'

'I didn't know you knew them.'

He looked at me rather strangely. He smiled. I didn't know what amused him.

'Oh, yes, I've known them for years. It's a very nice house to stay at.'

'Adolf is my nephew.'

'Sir Adolphus!'

'It suggests one of the bucks of the Regency, doesn't it? But I will not conceal from you that he was named Adolf.'

'Everyone I know calls him Freddy.'

'I know, and I understand that Miriam, his wife, only answers to the name of Muriel.'

'How does he happen to be your nephew?'

'Because Hannah Rabenstein, my sister, married Alfons Bleikogel, who ended life as Sir Alfred Bland, first Baronet, and Adolf, their only son, in due course became Sir Adolphus Bland, second Baronet.

'Then Freddy Bland's mother, the Lady Bland who lives in Portland Place, is your sister?'

'Yes, my sister Hannah. She was the eldest of the family. She's eighty, but in full possession of her faculties and a remarkable woman.'

'I've never met her.'

'I think your friends the Blands would just as soon you didn't. She has never lost her German accent.'

'Do you never see them?' I asked.

'I haven't spoken to them for twenty years. I am such a Jew and they are so English.' He smiled. 'I could never remember that their names were Freddy and Muriel. I used to come out with an Adolf or a Miriam at awkward moments. And they didn't like my stories. It was better that we should not meet. When the war broke out and I would not change my name it was the last straw. It was too late, I could never have accustomed my friends to think of me as anything but Ferdy Rabenstein; I was quite content. I was not ambitious to be a Smith, a Brown or a Robinson.'

Though he spoke facetiously, there was in his tone the faintest possible derision and I felt, hardly felt even, the sensation was so shadowy, that, as it had often vaguely seemed to me before, there was in the depth of his impenetrable heart a cynical contempt for the Gentiles he had conquered.

'Then you don't know the two boys?' I said.

'No.'

'The eldest is called George, you know. I don't think he's so clever as Harry, the other one, but he's an engaging youth. I think you'd like him.'

'Where is he now?'

'Well, he's just been sent down from Oxford. I suppose he's at home. Harry's still at Eton.'

'Why don't you bring George to lunch with me?'

'I'll ask him. I should think he'd love to come.'

'It has reached my ears that he's been a little troublesome.'

'Oh, I don't know. He wouldn't go into the army, which is what they wanted. They rather fancied the Guards. And so he went to Oxford instead. He didn't work and he spent a great deal of money and he painted the town red. It was all quite normal.'

'What was he sent down for?'

'I don't know. Nothing of any consequence.'

At that moment our host rose and we went upstairs. When Ferdy bade me good night he asked me not to forget about his great-nephew.

'Ring me up,' he said. 'Wednesday would suit me. Or Friday.'

Next day I went down to Tilby. It was an Elizabethan mansion standing in a spacious park, in which roamed fallow deer, and from its windows you had wide views of rolling downs. It seemed to me that as far as the eye could reach the land belonged to the Blands. His tenants must have found Sir Adolphus a wonderful landlord, for I never saw farms kept in such order, the barns and cow-sheds were spick and span and the pigsties were a picture; the public houses looked like Old English water-colours and the cottages he had built on the estate combined admirably picturesqueness and convenience. It must have cost him a pot of money to run the place on these lines. Fortunately he had it. The park with its grand old trees (and its nine-hole golf course) was tended like a garden, and the wide-

stretching gardens were the pride of the neighbourhood. The magnificent house, with its steep roofs and mullioned windows, had been
restored by the most celebrated architect in England and furnished
by Lady Bland, with taste and knowledge, in a style that perfectly
fitted it.

'Of course it's very simple,' she said. 'Just an English house in the
country.'

The dining-room was adorned with old English sporting pictures
and the Chippendale chairs were of incredible value. In the drawing-
room were portraits by Reynolds and Gainsborough and landscapes
by Old Crome and Richard Wilson. Even in my bedroom with its
four-post bed were water-colours by Birket Foster. It was very
beautiful and a treat to stay there, but though it would have
distressed Muriel Bland beyond anything to know it, it entirely
missed oddly enough the effect she had sought. It did not give you
for a moment the impression of an English house. You had the feeling
that every object had been bought with a careful eye to the general
scheme. You missed the full Academy portraits that hung in the
dining-room beside a Carlo Dolci that an ancestor had brought back
from the Grand Tour, and the water-colours painted by a great-aunt
that cluttered up the drawing-room so engagingly. There was no
ugly Victorian sofa that had always been there and that it never
occurred to anybody to take away and no needlework chairs that an
unmarried daughter had so painstakingly worked at about the time
of the Great Exhibition. There was beauty but no sentiment.

And yet how comfortable it was and how well looked after you
were! And what a cordial greeting the Blands gave you! They seemed
really to like people. They were generous and kindly. They were
never happier than when they were entertaining the county, and
though they had not owned the property for more than twenty
years they had established themselves firmly in the favour of their
neighbours. Except perhaps in their splendour and the competent

way in which the estate was run there was nothing to suggest that they had not been settled there for centuries.

Freddy had been at Eton and Oxford. He was now in the early fifties. He was quiet in manner, courtly, very clever, I imagine, but a trifle reserved. He had great elegance, but it was not an English elegance; he had grey hair and a short pointed grey beard, fine dark eyes and an aquiline nose. He was just above middle height; I don't think you would have taken him for a Jew, but rather for a foreign diplomat of some distinction. He was a man of character, but gave you, strangely enough, notwithstanding the success he had had in life, an impression of faint melancholy. His successes had been financial and political; in the world of sport, for all his perseverance, he had never shone. For many years he had followed hounds, but he was a bad rider and I think it must have been a relief to him when he could persuade himself that middle age and pressure of business forced him to give up hunting. He had excellent shooting and gave grand parties for it, but he was a poor shot; and despite the course in his park he never succeeded in being more than an indifferent golfer. He knew only too well how much these things meant in England and his incapacity was a bitter disappointment to him. However George would make up for it.

George was scratch at golf, and though tennis was not his game he played much better than the average; the Blands had had him taught to shoot as soon as he was old enough to hold a gun and he was a fine shot; they had put him on a pony when he was two, and Freddy, watching him mount his horse, knew that out hunting when the boy came to a fence he felt exhilaration and not that sickening feeling in the pit of his stomach, which, though he had chased the fox with such grim determination, had always made the sport a torture to him. George was so tall and slim, his curly hair, of a palish brown, was so fine, his eyes were so blue, he was the perfect type of the young Englishman. He had the engaging candour of the breed. His nose was straight, though perhaps a trifle fleshy, and his lips were perhaps a little full and sensual, but he had beautiful teeth, and his smooth skin was like ivory. George was the apple of his father's eye. He did not like Harry, his second son, so well. He was rather stocky, broad-shouldered and strong for his age, but his black eyes, shining with cleverness, his coarse dark hair, and his big nose revealed his race. Freddy was severe with him, and often impatient, but with George he was all indulgence. Harry would go into the business, he had brains and push, but George was the heir. George would be an English gentleman.

George had offered to motor me down in the roadster his father had given him as a birthday present. He drove very fast and we arrived before the rest of the guests. The Blands were sitting on the lawn and tea was laid out under a magnificent cedar.

'By the way,' I said presently, 'I saw Ferdy Rabenstein the other day and he wants me to bring George to lunch with him.'

I had not mentioned the invitation to George on the way because I thought that if there had been a family coldness I had better address his parents as well.

'Who in God's name is Ferdy Rabenstein?' said George.

How brief is human glory! A generation back such a question would have seemed grotesque.

'He's by way of being your great-uncle,' I replied.

A glance had passed from father to mother when I first spoke.

'He's a horrid old man,' said Muriel.

'I don't think it's in the least necessary for George to resume relationships that were definitely severed before he was born,' said Freddy with decision.

'Anyhow I've delivered the message,' said I, feeling somewhat snubbed.

'I don't want to see the old blighter,' said George.

The conversation was broken off by the arrival of other guests and in a little while George went off to play golf with one of his Oxford friends.

It was not until next day that the matter was referred to again. I had played an unsatisfactory round with Freddy Bland in the morning and several sets of what is known as country-house tennis in the afternoon and was sitting along with Muriel on the terrace. In England we have so much bad weather that it is only fair that a beautiful day should be more beautiful than anywhere in the world and this June evening was perfect. The blue sky was cloudless and the air was balmy; before us stretched green rolling downs, and woods, and in the distance you saw the red roofs of a little village church. It was a day when to be alive was sufficient happiness. Detached lines of poetry hovered vaguely in my memory. Muriel and I had been chatting desultorily.

'I hope you didn't think it rather horrid of us to refuse to let George lunch with Ferdy,' she said suddenly. 'He's such a fearful snob, isn't he?'

'Do you think so? He's always been very nice to me.'

'We haven't been on speaking terms for twenty years. Freddy never forgave him for his behaviour during the war. So unpatriotic, I thought, and one really must draw the line somewhere. You know, he absolutely refused to drop his horrible German name, With Freddy in Parliament and running munitions and all that sort of thing it was quite impossible. I don't know why he should want to see George. He can't mean anything to him.'

'He's an old man. George and Harry are his great-nephews. He must leave his money to someone.'

'We'd rather not have his money,' said Muriel coldly.

Of course I didn't care a row of pins whether George went to lunch with Ferdy Rabenstein, and I was quite willing to let the matter drop, but evidently the Blands had talked it over and Muriel felt that some explanation was due to me.

'Of course you know that Freddy has Jewish blood in him,' she said.

She looked at me sharply. Muriel was rather a big blonde woman and she spent a great deal of time trying to keep down the corpulence to which she was predisposed. She had been very pretty when young, and even now was a comely person; but her round blue eyes, slightly prominent, her fleshy nose, the shape of her face and the back of her neck, her exuberant manner, betrayed her race. No English woman, however fair-haired, ever looked like that. And yet her observation was designed to make me take it for granted that she was a Gentile. I answered discreetly:

'So many people have nowadays.'

'I know. But there's no reason to dwell on it, is there? After all, we're absolutely English; no one could be more English than George, in appearance and manner and everything; I mean, he's such a fine sportsman and all that sort of thing, I can't see any object of his knowing Jews just because they happen to be distant connexions of his.'

'It's very difficult in England now not to know Jews, isn't it?'

'Oh, I know, in London one does meet a good many, and I think some of them are very nice. They're so artistic. I don't go so far as to say that Freddy and I deliberately avoid them, of course I wouldn't do that, but it just happens that we don't really know any of them very well. And down here, there simply aren't any to know.

I could not but admire the convincing manner in which she spoke. It would not have surprised me to be told that she really believed every word she said.

'You said that Ferdy might leave George his money. Well, I don't believe it's so very much anyway; it was quite a comfortable fortune before the war, but that's nothing nowadays. Besides we're hoping that George will go in for politics when he's a little older, and I don't think it would do him any good in the constituency to inherit money from a Mr Rabenstein.'

'Is George interested in politics?' I asked, to change the conversation.

'Oh, I do hope so. After all, there's the family constituency waiting for him. It's a safe Conservative seat and one can't expect Freddy to go on with the grind of the House of Commons indefinitely.'

Muriel was grand. She talked already of the constituency as though twenty generations of Blands had sat for it. Her remark, however, was my first intimation that Freddy's ambition was not satisfied.

'I suppose Freddy would go to the House of Lords when George was old enough to stand.'

'We've done a good deal for the party,' said Muriel.

Muriel was a Catholic and she often told you that she had been educated in a convent – 'Such sweet women, those nuns, I always said that if I had a daughter I should have sent her to a convent too' – but she liked her servants to be Church of England, and on Sunday evenings we had what was called supper because the fish was cold and there was ice-cream, so that they could go to church, and we were waited on by two footmen instead of four. It was still light when we finished and Freddy and I, smoking our cigars, walked up and down the terrace in the gloaming. I suppose Muriel had told him of her conversation with me, and it may be that his refusal to let George see his great-uncle still troubled him, but being subtler than she he attacked the question more indirectly. He told me that he had been very much worried about George. It had been a great disappointment that he had refused to go into the army.

'I should have thought he'd have loved the life,' he said.

'And he would certainly have looked marvellous in his Guards uniform.'

'He would, wouldn't he?' returned Freddy, ingenuously. 'I wonder he could resist that.'

He had been completely idle at Oxford; although his father had given him a very large allowance, he had got monstrously into debt; and now he had been sent down. But though he spoke so tartly I could see that he was not a little proud of his scapegrace son, he loved him with oh, such an unEnglish love, and in his heart it flattered him that George had cut such a dash.

'Why should you worry?' I said. 'You don't really care if George has a degree or not.'

Freddy chuckled.

'No, I don't suppose I do really. I always think the only important thing about Oxford is that people know you were there, and I dare say that George isn't any wilder than the other young men in his set. It's the future I'm thinking of. He's so damned idle. He doesn't seem to want to do anything but have a good time.'

'He's young, you know.'

'He's not interested in politics, and though he's so good at games he's not even very keen on sport. He seems to spend most of his time strumming the piano.'

'That's a harmless amusement.'

'Oh, yes, I don't mind that, but he can't go on loafing indefinitely. You see, all this will be his one day.' Freddy gave a sweeping gesture that seemed to embrace the whole country, but I knew that he did not own it all yet. 'I'm very anxious that he should be fit to assume his responsibilities. His mother is very ambitious for him, but I only want him to be an English gentleman.'

Freddy gave me a sidelong glance as though he wanted to say something but hesitated in case I thought it ridiculous; but there is one advantage in being a writer that, since people look upon you as of no account, they will often say things to you that they would not to their equals. He thought he would risk it.

'You know, I've got an idea that nowhere in the world now is the Greek ideal of life so perfectly cultivated as by the English country gentleman living on his estates. I think his life has the beauty of a work of art.'

I could not but smile when I reflected that it was impossible for the English country gentleman in these days to do anything of the sort without a packet of money safely invested in American Bonds, but I smiled with sympathy. I thought it rather touching that this Jewish financier should cherish so romantic a dream.

'I want him to be a good landlord. I want him to take his part in the affairs of the country. I want him to be a thorough sportsman.'

'Poor mutt,' I thought, but said: 'Well, what are your plans for George now?'

'I think he has a fancy for the diplomatic service. He's suggested going to Germany to learn the language.'

'A very good idea, I should have thought.'

'For some reason he's got it into his head that he wants to go to Munich.'

'A nice place.'

Next day I went back to London and shortly after my arrival rang up Ferdy.

'I'm sorry, but George isn't able to come to lunch on Wednesday.'

'What about Friday?'

'Friday's no good either.' I thought it useless to beat about the bush. 'The fact is, his people aren't keen on his lunching with you.'

There was a moment's silence. Then:

'I see. Well, will you come on Wednesday anyway?'

'Yes, I'd like to,' I answered.

So on Wednesday at half past one I strolled round to Curzon Street. Ferdy received me with the somewhat elaborate graciousness that he had cultivated. He made no reference to the Blands. We sat in the drawing-room and I could not help reflecting what an eye for beautiful objects that family had. The room was more crowded than the fashion of today approves, and the gold snuff-boxes in vitrines, the French china, appealed to a taste that was not mine, but they were no doubt choice pieces; and the Louis XV suite, with its beautiful *petit point*, must have been worth an enormous lot of money. The pictures on the wall by Lancret, Pater and Watteau did not greatly interest me, but I recognized their intrinsic excellence. It was a proper setting for this aged man of the world. It fitted his period. Suddenly the door opened and George was announced. Ferdy saw my surprise and gave me a little smile of triumph.

'I'm very glad you were able to come after all,' he said as he shook George's hand.

I saw him in a glance take in his great-nephew whom he saw today for the first time. George was very well dressed. He wore a short black coat, striped trousers, and the grey double-breasted waistcoat which at that time was the mode. You could only wear it with elegance if you were tall and thin and your belly was slightly concave. I felt sure that Ferdy knew exactly who George's tailor was and what haberdasher he went to and approved of them. George, so smart and trim, wearing his clothes so beautifully, certainly looked very handsome. We went down to luncheon. Ferdy had the social graces at his fingers' ends and he put the boy at his ease, but I saw that he was carefully appraising him; then, I do not know why, he began to tell some of his Jewish stories. He told them with gusto and with all his wonderful mimicry. I saw George flush, and though he laughed at them, I could see that it was with embarrassment. I wondered what on earth had induced Ferdy to be so tactless. But he was watching George and he told story after story. It looked as though he would never stop. I wondered if for some reason I could not grasp he was taking a malicious pleasure in the boy's obvious discomfiture. At last we went upstairs and to make things easier I asked Ferdy to play the piano. He played us three or four little waltzes. He had lost none of his exquisite lightness nor his sense of their lilting rhythm. Then he turned to George.

'Do you play?' he asked him.

'A little.'

'Won't you play something?'

'I'm afraid I only play classical music. I don't think it would interest you.'

Ferdy smiled slightly, but did not insist. I said it was time for me to go and George accompanied me.

'What a filthy old Jew,' he said as soon as we were in the street. 'I hated those stories of his.'

'They're his great stunt. He always tells them.'

'Would you if you were a Jew?'

I shrugged my shoulders

'How is it that you came to lunch after all?' I asked George.

He chuckled. He was a light-hearted creature, with a sense of humour, and he shook off the irritation his great-uncle had caused him.

'He went to see Granny. You don't know Granny, do you?'

'No.'

'She treats daddy like a kid in Etons. Granny said I was to go to lunch with great-uncle Ferdy and what Granny says goes.'

'I see.'

A week or so later George went to Munich to learn German. I happened then to go on a journey and it was not till the following spring that I was again in London. Soon after my arrival I found myself sitting next to Muriel Bland at dinner. I asked after George.

'He's still in Germany,' she said.

'I see in the papers that you're going to have a great beano at Tilby for his coming of age.'

'We're going to entertain the tenants and they're making George a presentation.'

She was less exuberant than usual, but I did not pay much attention to the fact. She led a strenuous life and it might be that she was tired. I knew she liked to talk of her son, so I continued.

'I suppose George has been having a grand time in Germany,' I said.

She did not answer for a moment and I gave her a glance. I was surprised to see that her eyes were filled with tears.

'I'm afraid George has gone mad,' she said.

'What *do* you mean?'

'We've been so frightfully worried. Freddy's so angry, he won't even discuss it. I don't know what we are going to do.'

Of course it immediately occurred to me that George who, I supposed, like most young Englishmen sent to learn the language, had been put with a German family, had fallen in love with the daughter of the house and wanted to marry her. I had a pretty strong suspicion that the Blands were intent on his making a very grand marriage.

'Why, what's happened?' I asked.

'He wants to become a pianist.'

'A what?'

'A professional pianist.'

'What on earth put that idea in his head?'

'Heaven knows. We didn't know anything about it. We thought he was working for his exam. I went out to see him. I thought I'd like to know that he was getting on all right. Oh, my dear. He looks like nothing on earth. And he used to be so smart; I could have cried. He told me he wasn't going in for the exam, and had never had any intention of doing so; he'd only suggested the diplomatic service so that we'd let him go to Germany and he'd be able to study music.'

'But has he any talent?'

'Oh, that's neither here nor there. Even if he had the genius of Paderewski we couldn't have George traipsing around the country playing at concerts. No one can deny that I'm very artistic, and so is Freddy, we love music and we've always known a lot of artists, but George will have a very great position, it's out of the question. We've set our hearts on his going into Parliament. He'll be very rich one day. There's nothing he can't aspire to.'

'Did you point all that out to him?'

'Of course I did. He laughed at me. I told him he'd break his father's heart. He said his father could always fall back on Harry. Of course I'm devoted to Harry, and he's as clever as a monkey, but it was always understood that he was to go into the business; even though I am his mother I can see that he hasn't got the advantages that George has. Do you know what he said to me? He said that if his father would settle five pounds a week on him he would resign everything in Harry's favour and Harry could be his father's heir and succeed to the baronetcy and everything. It's too ridiculous. He said that if the Crown Prince of Roumania could abdicate a throne he didn't see why he couldn't abdicate his baronetcy. But you can't do that. Nothing can prevent him from being third baronet and if Freddy should be granted a peerage from succeeding to it at Freddy's death. Do you know, he even wants to drop the name of Bland and take some horrible German name.'

I could not help asking what.

'Bleikogel or something like that,' she answered.

That was a name I recognized. I remembered Ferdy telling me that Hannah Rabenstein had married Alfons Bleikogel who became eventually Sir Alfred Bland, first Baronet. It was all very strange. I wondered what had happened to the charming, so typically English boy I had seen only a few months before.

'Of course when I came home and told Freddy he was furious. I've never seen him so angry. He foamed at the mouth. He wired George to come back immediately and George wired back to say he couldn't on account of his work.'

'Is he working?'

'From morning till night. That's the maddening part of it. He never did a stroke of work in his life. Freddy used to say he was born idle.'

'H'm.'

'Then Freddy wired to say that if he didn't come he'd stop his allowance and George wired back: "Stop it." That put the lid on. You don't know what Freddy can be when his back is up.'

I knew that Freddy had inherited a large fortune, but I knew also that he had immensely increased it, and I could well imagine that behind the courteous and amiable Squire of Tilby there was a ruthless man of affairs. He had been used to having his own way and I could believe that when crossed he would be hard and cruel.

'We'd been making George a very handsome allowance, but you know how frightfully extravagant he was. We didn't think he'd be able to hold out long and in point of fact within a month he wrote to Ferdy and asked him to lend him a hundred pounds. Ferdy went to my mother-in-law, she's his sister, you know, and asked her what it meant. Though they hadn't spoken for twenty years Freddy went to see him and begged him not to send George a penny, and he promised he wouldn't. I don't know how George has been making both ends meet. I'm sure Freddy's right, but I can't help being rather worried. If I hadn't given Freddy any word of honour that I wouldn't send him anything I think I'd have slipped a few notes in a letter in case of accident. I mean, it's awful to think that perhaps he hasn't got enough to eat.'

'It'll do him no harm to go short for a bit.'

'We were in an awful hole, you know. We'd made all sorts of preparations for his coming of age, and I'd issued hundreds of invitations. Suddenly George said he wouldn't come. I was simply frantic. I wrote and wired. I would have gone to Germany only Freddy wouldn't let me. I mean, it's the sort of thing it's so difficult to explain. Then my mother-in-law stepped in. You don't know her, do you? She's an extraordinary old woman. You'd never think she was Freddy's mother. She was German originally, but of very good family.'

'Oh?'

'To tell you the truth I'm rather frightened of her. She tackled Freddy and then she wrote to George herself. She said that if he'd come home for his twenty-first birthday she'd pay any debts he had in Munich and we'd all give a patient hearing to anything he had to say. He agreed to that and we're expecting him one day next week. But I'm not looking forward to it, I can tell you.'

She gave a deep sigh. When we were walking upstairs after dinner Freddy addressed me.

'I see Muriel has been telling you about George. The damned fool! I have no patience with him. Fancy wanting to be a pianist. It's so ungentlemanly.'

'He's very young, you know,' I said soothingly.

'He's had things too easy for him. I've been much too indulgent. There's never been a thing he wanted that I haven't given him. I'll learn him.'

The Blands had a discreet apprehension of the uses of advertisement and I gathered from the papers that the celebrations at Tilby of George's twenty-first birthday were conducted in accordance with the usage of English country families. There was a dinner-party and a ball for the gentry and a collation and dance in marquees on the lawn for the tenants. Expensive bands were brought down from London. In the illustrated papers were pictures of George surrounded by his family being presented with a solid silver tea-set by the tenantry. They had subscribed to have his portrait painted, but since his absence from the country had made it impossible for him to sit, the tea-service had been substituted. I read in the columns of the gossip writers that his father had given him a hunter, his mother a gramophone that changed its own records, his grandmother the dowager Lady Bland an *Encyclopaedia Britannica*, and his great uncle Ferdinand Rabenstein a *Virgin and Child* by Pellegrino da Modena. I could not help observing that these gifts were bulky and not readily convertible into cash. From Ferdy's presence at the festivities I concluded that George's unaccountable vagary had effected a reconciliation between uncle and nephew. I was right. Ferdy did not at all like the notion of his great-nephew becoming a professional pianist. At the first hint of danger to its prestige the family drew together and a united front was presented to oppose George's designs. Since I was not there I only know from hearsay what happened when the birthday celebrations were over. Ferdy told me something and so did Muriel, and later George gave me his version. The Blands had very much the impression that when George came home and found himself occupying the centre of the stage, when, surrounded by splendour, he saw for himself once more how much it meant to be the heir of a great estate, he would weaken. They surrounded him with love. They flattered him. They hung on his words. They counted on the goodness of his heart and thought that if they were kind to him he would not have the courage to cause them pain. They seemed to take it for granted that he had no intention of going back to Germany and in conversation included him in all their plans. George did not say very much. He seemed to be enjoying himself. He did not open a piano. Things looked as though they were going very well. Peace descended on the troubled house. Then one day at luncheon when they were discussing a garden party to which they had all been asked for one day of the following week, George said pleasantly:

'Don't count on me. I shan't be here.'

'Oh, George, why not?' asked his mother.

'I must get back to my work. I'm leaving for Munich on Monday.'

There was an awful pause. Everyone looked for something to say, but was afraid of saying the wrong thing, and at last it seemed impossible to break it. Luncheon was finished in silence. Then George went into the garden and the others, old Lady Bland and Ferdy, Muriel and Sir Adolphus, into the morning-room. There was a family council. Muriel wept. Freddy flew into a temper. Presently from the drawing-room they heard the sound of someone playing a nocturne of Chopin. It was George. It was as though now he had announced his decision he had gone for comfort, rest, and strength to the instrument he loved. Freddy sprang to his feet.

'Stop that noise,' he cried. 'I won't have him play the piano in my house.'

Muriel rang for a servant and gave him a message.

'Will you tell Mr Bland that her ladyship has a bad headache and would he mind not playing the piano.'

Ferdy, the man of the world, was deputed to have a talk with George. He was authorized to make him certain promises if he would give up the idea of becoming a pianist. If he did not wish to go into the diplomatic service his father would not insist, but if he would stand for Parliament he was prepared to pay his election expenses, give him a flat in London, and make him an allowance of five thousand a year. I must say it was a handsome offer. I do not know what Ferdy said to the boy. I suppose he painted to him the life that a young man could lead in London on such an income. I am sure he made it very alluring. It availed nothing. All George asked was five pounds a week to be able to continue his studies and to be left alone. He was indifferent to the position that he might some day enjoy. He didn't want to hunt. He didn't want to shoot. He didn't want to be a Member of Parliament. He didn't want to be a millionaire. He didn't want to be a baronet. He didn't want to be a peer. Ferdy left him defeated and in a state of considerable exasperation.

After dinner that evening there was a battle royal. Freddy was a quick-tempered man, unused to opposition, and he gave George the rough side of his tongue. I gather that it was very rough indeed. The women who sought to restrain his violence were sternly silenced. Perhaps for the first time in his life Freddy would not listen to his mother. George was obstinate and sullen. He had made up his mind

and if his father didn't like it he could lump it. Freddy was peremp-
tory. He forbade George to go back to Germany. George answered
that he was twenty-one and his own master. He would go where he
chose. Freddy swore he would not give him a penny.

'All right, I'll earn money.'

'You! You've never done a stroke of work in your life. What do you
expect to do to earn money?'

'Sell old clothes,' grinned George.

There was a gasp from all of them. Muriel was so taken aback that
she said a stupid thing.

'Like a Jew?'

'Well, aren't I a Jew? And aren't you a Jewess and isn't daddy a
Jew? We're all Jews, the whole gang of us, and everyone knows it and
what the hell's the good of pretending we're not?'

Then a very dreadful thing happened. Freddy burst suddenly into
tears. I'm afraid he didn't behave very much like Sir Adolphus Bland,
Bart, M.P., and the good old English gentleman he so much wanted
to be, but like an emotional Adolf Bleikogel who loved his son and
wept with mortification because the great hopes he had set on him
were brought to nothing and the ambition of his life was frustrated.
He cried noisily with great loud sobs and pulled his beard and beat
his breast and rocked to and fro. Then they all began to cry, old
Lady Bland and Muriel, and Ferdy, who sniffed and blew his nose
and wiped the tears streaming down his face, and even George cried.
Of course it was very painful, but to our rough Anglo-Saxon
temperament I am afraid it must seem also a trifle ridiculous. No one
tried to console anybody else. They just sobbed and sobbed. It broke
up the party.

But it had no result on the situation. George remained obdurate.
His father would not speak to him. There were more scenes. Muriel
sought to excite his pity; he was deaf to her piteous entreaties, he
did not seem to mind if he broke her heart, he did not care two

hoots if he killed his father. Ferdy appealed to him as a sportsman and a man of the world. George was flippant and indeed personally offensive. Old Lady Bland with her guttural German accent and strong common sense argued with him, but he would not listen to reason. It was she, however, who at last found a way out. She made George acknowledge that it was no use to throw away all the beautiful things the world laid at his feet unless he had talent. It was not worth while to be a second rate pianist. His only excuse, his only justification, was genius. If he had genius his family had no right to stand in his way.

'You can't expect me to show genius already,' said George. 'I shall have to work for years.'

'Are you sure you are prepared for that?'

'It's my only wish in the world. I'll work like a dog. I only want to be given my chance.'

This was the proposition she made. His father was determined to give him nothing and obviously they could not let the boy starve. He had mentioned five pounds a week. Well, she was willing to give him that herself. He could go back to Germany and study for two years. At the end of that time he must come back and they would get some competent and disinterested person to hear him play, and if then that person said he showed promise of becoming a first-rate pianist no further obstacles would be placed in his way. He would be given every advantage, help, and encouragement. If on the other hand that person decided that his natural gifts were not such as to ensure ultimate success he must promise faithfully to give up all thoughts of making music his profession and in every way accede to his father's wishes. George could hardly believe his ears.

'Do you mean that, Granny?'

'I do.'

'But will daddy agree?'

'I vill see dat he does,' she answered.

George seized her in his arms and impetuously kissed her on both cheeks.

'Darling,' he cried.

'Ah, but de promise?'

He gave her his solemn word of honour that he would faithfully abide by the terms of the arrangement. Two days later he went back to Germany. Though his father consented unwillingly to his going, and indeed could not help doing so, he would not be reconciled to him and when he left refused to say good-bye to him.

I imagine that in no manner could he have caused himself such pain. I permit myself a trite remark. It is strange that men, inhabitants for so short a while of an alien and inhuman world, should go out of their way to cause themselves so much unhappiness.

George had stipulated that during his two years of study his family should not visit him, so that when Muriel heard some months before he was due to come home that I was passing through Munich on my way to Vienna, whither business called me, it was not unnatural that she should ask me to look him up. She was anxious to have first-hand information about him. She gave me George's address and I wrote ahead, telling him I was spending a day in Munich, and asked him to lunch with me. His answer awaited me at the hotel. He said he worked all day and could not spare the time to lunch with me, but if I would come to his studio about six he would like to show me that and if I had nothing better to do would love to spend the evening with me. So soon after six I went to the address he gave me. He lived on the second floor of a large block of flats and when I came to his door I heard the sound of piano-playing. It stopped when I rang and George opened the door for me. I hardly recognized him. He had grown very fat. His hair was extremely long, it curled all over his head in picturesque confusion; and he had certainly not shaved for three days. He wore a grimy pair of Oxford bags, a tennis shirt, and slippers. He was not very clean and his finger-nails were rimmed with black. It was a startling change from the spruce, slim youth so elegantly dressed in such beautiful clothes that I had last seen. I could not but think it would be a shock to Ferdy to see him now. The studio was large and bare; on the walls were three of four unframed canvases of a highly cubist nature, there were several arm-chairs much the worse for wear, and a grand piano. Books were littered about and old newspapers and art magazines. It was dirty and untidy and there was a frowsy smell of stale beer and stale smoke.

'Do you live here alone?' I asked.

'Yes, I have a woman who comes in twice a week and cleans up. But I make my own breakfast and lunch.'

'Can you cook?'

'Oh, I only have bread and cheese and a bottle of beer for lunch. I dine at *Bierstube*.'

It was pleasant to discover that he was very glad to see me. He seemed in great spirits and extremely happy. He asked after his relations and we talked of one thing and another. He had a lesson twice a week and for the rest of the time practised. He told me that he worked ten hours a day.

'That's a change,' I said.

He laughed.

'Daddy said I was born tired. I wasn't really lazy. I didn't see the use of working at things that bored me.'

I asked him how he was getting on with the piano. He seemed to be satisfied with his progress and I begged him to play to me.

'Oh, not now, I'm all in, I've been at it all day. Let's go out and dine and come back here later and then I'll play. I generally go to the same place, there are several students I know there, and it's rather fun.'

Presently we set out. He put on socks and shoes and a very old golf coat, and we walked together through the wide quiet streets. It was a brisk cold day. His step was buoyant. He looked round him with a sigh of delight.

'I love Munich,' he said. 'It's the only city in the world where there's art in the very air you breathe. After all, art is the only thing that matters, isn't it. I loathe the idea of going home.'

'All the same I'm afraid you have to.'

'I know. I'll go all right, but I'm not going to think about it till the time comes.'

'When you do, you might do worse than get a haircut. If you don't mind my saying so you look almost too artistic to be convincing.'

'You English, you're such Philistines,' he said.

He took me to a rather large restaurant in a side street, crowded even at that early hour with people dining, and furnished heavily in the German medieval style. A table covered with a red cloth, well away from the air, was reserved for George and his friends and when we went to it four or five youths were at it. There was a Pole studying Oriental languages, a student of philosophy, a painter (I suppose the author of George's cubist pictures), a Swede, and a young man who introduced himself to me, clicking his heels, as Hans Reiting, *Dichter*, namely Hans Reiting, poet. Not one of them was more than twenty-two and I felt a trifle out of it. They all addressed George as *du* and I noticed that his German was extremely fluent. I had not spoken it for some time and mine was rusty, so that I could not take much part of the lively conversation. But nevertheless I thoroughly enjoyed myself. They ate sparingly, but drank a good deal of beer. They talked of art and women. They were very revolutionary and though gay very much in earnest. They were contemptuous of everyone you had ever heard of, and the only point on which they all agreed was that in this topsy-turvy world only the vulgar could hope for success. They argued points of technique with animation, and contradicted one another, and shouted and were obscene. They had a grand time.

At about eleven George and I walked back to his studio. Munich is a city that frolics demurely and except about the Marienplatz the streets were still and empty. When we got in he took off his coat and said:

'Now I'll play to you.'

I sat in one of the dilapidated arm-chairs and a broken spring stuck into my behind, but I made myself as comfortable as I could. George played Chopin. I know very little of music and that is one of the reasons for which I have found this story difficult to write. When I go to a concert at the Queen's Hall and in the intervals read the programme it is all Greek to me. I know nothing of harmony and counterpoint. I shall never forget how humiliated I felt once when, having come to Munich for a Wagner festival, I went to a wonderful performance of *Tristan und Isolde* and never heard a note of it. The first few bars sent me off and I began to think of what I was writing, my characters leapt into life and I heard their long conversations, I suffered their pains and was a party to their joy; the years swept by and all sorts of things happened to me, the spring brought me its rapture and in the winter I was cold and hungry; and I loved and I hated and I died. I suppose there were intervals in which I walked round and round the garden and probably ate *Schinken-Brödchen* and drank beer, but I have no recollection of them. The only thing I know is that when the curtain for the last time fell I woke with a start. I had had a wonderful time, but I could not help thinking it was very stupid of me to come such a long way and spend so much money if I couldn't pay attention to what I heard and saw.

I knew most of the things George played. They were the familiar pieces of concert programmes. He played with a great deal of dash. Then he played Beethoven's *Appassionata*. I used to play it myself when I played the piano (very badly) in my far distant youth and I still knew every note of it. Of course it is a classic and a great work, it would be foolish to deny it, but I confess that at this time of day it leaves me cold. It is like *Paradise Lost*, splendid, but a trifle stolid. This too George played with vigour. He sweated profusely. At first I could not make out what was the matter with his playing, something did not seem to me quite right, and then it struck me that the two hands did not exactly synchronize, so that there was ever so slight an interval between the bass and the treble; but I repeat, I am ignorant of these things; what disconcerted me might have been merely the effect of his having drunk a good deal of beer that evening or indeed only my fancy. I said all I could think of to praise him.

'Of course I know I need a lot more work. I'm only a beginner, but I know I can do it. I feel it in my bones. It'll take me ten years, but then I shall be a pianist.'

He was tired and came away from the piano. It was after midnight and I suggested going, but he would not hear of it. He opened a couple of bottles of beer and lit his pipe. He wanted to talk.

'Are you happy here?' I asked him.

'Very,' he answered gravely. 'I'd like to stay here for ever. I've never had such fun in my life. This evening, for instance. Wasn't it grand?'

'It was very jolly. But one can't go on leading the student's life. Your friends here will grow older and go away.'

'Others'll come. There are always students here and people like that.'

'Yes, but you'll grow older too. Is there anything more lamentable than the middle-aged man who tries to go on living the under-graduate's life? The old fellow who wants to be a boy amongst boys, and tries to persuade himself that they'll accept him as one of them-selves – how ridiculous he is. It can't be done.'

'I feel so at home here. My poor father wants me to be an English gentleman. It gives me gooseflesh. I'm not a sportsman. I don't care a damn for hunting and shooting and playing cricket. I was only acting.'

'You gave a very natural performance.'

'It wasn't till I came here that I knew it wasn't real. I loved Eton, and Oxford was a riot, but all the same I knew I didn't belong.

I played the part all right, because acting's in my blood, but there was always something in me that wasn't satisfied. The house in Grosvenor Square is a freehold and daddy paid a hundred and eighty thousand pounds for Tilby; I don't know if you understand what I mean, I felt they were just furnished houses we'd taken for the season and one of these days we'd pack up and the real owners would come back.'

I listened to him attentively, but I wondered how much he was describing what he had obscurely felt and how much he imagined now in his changed circumstances that he had felt.

'I used to hate hearing great-uncle Ferdy tell his Jewish stories. I thought it so damned mean. I understand now; it was a safety valve. My God, the strain of being a man about town. It's easier for daddy, he can play the old English squire at Tilby, but in the City he can be himself. He's all right. I've taken the make-up off and my stage clothes and at last I can be my real self too. What a relief! You know, I don't like English people. I never really know where I am with you. You're so dull and conventional. You never let yourselves go. There's no freedom in you, freedom of the soul, and you're such funks. There's nothing in the world you're so frightened of as doing the wrong thing.'

'Don't forget that you're English yourself, George,' I murmured.

He laughed.

'I? I'm not English. I haven't got a drop of English blood in me. I'm a Jew and you know it, and a German Jew into the bargain. I don't want to be English. I want to be a Jew. My friends are Jews. You don't know how much more easy I feel with them. I can be myself. We did everything we could to avoid Jews at home. Mummy, because she was blonde, thought she could get away with it and pretended she was a Gentile. What rot! D'you know, I have a lot a fun wandering about the Jewish parts of Munich and looking at the people. I went to Frankfurt once, there are a lot of them there, and

I walked about and looked at the frowzy old men with their hooked noses and the fat women with their false hair. I felt such a sympathy for them, I felt I belonged to them, I could have kissed them. When they looked at me I wondered if they knew that I was one of them. I wish to God I knew Yiddish. I'd like to become friends with them, and go into their houses and eat Kosher food and all that sort of thing. I wanted to go to a synagogue, but I was afraid I'd do the wrong thing and be kicked out. I like the smell of the Ghetto and the sense of life, and the mystery and the dust and the squalor and the romance. I shall never get the longing for it out of my head now. That's the real thing. All the rest is pretence.'

'You'll break your father's heart,' I said.

'It's his or mine. Why can't he let me go? There's Harry. Harry would love to be squire of Tilby. He'd be an English gentleman all right. You know, mummy's set her heart on my marrying a Christian. Harry would love to. He'll found the good old English family all right. After all, I ask so little. I only want five pounds a week, and they can keep the title and the park and the Gainsboroughs and the whole bag of tricks.'

'Well, the fact remains that you gave your solemn word of honour to go back after two years.'

'I'll go back all right,' he said sullenly. 'Lea Makart has promised to come and hear me play.'

'What'll you do if she says you're no good?'

'Shoot myself,' he said gaily.

'What nonsense,' I answered in the same tone.

'Do you feel at home in England?'

'No,' I said, 'but then I don't feel at home anywhere else.'

But he was quite naturally not interested in me.

'I loathe the idea of going back. Now that I know what life has to offer I wouldn't be an English country gentleman for anything in the world. My God, the boredom of it!'

73

'Money's a very nice thing and I've always understood it's very pleasant to be an English peer.'

'Money means nothing to me. I want none of the things it can buy, and I don't happen to be a snob.'

It was growing very late and I had to get up early next day. It seemed unnecessary for me to pay too much attention to what George said. It was the sort of nonsense a young man might very well indulge in when thrown suddenly among painters and poets. Art is strong wine and needs a strong head to carry it. The divine fire burns most efficiently in those who temper its fury with horse sense. After all, George was not twenty-three yet. Time teaches. And when all was said and done his future was no concern of mine. I bade him good night and walked back to my hotel. The stars were shining in the indifferent sky. I left Munich in the morning.

I did not tell Muriel on my return to London what George had said to me, or what he looked like, but contented myself with assuring her that he was well and happy, working very hard, and seemed to be leading a virtuous and sober life. Six months later he came home. Muriel asked me to go down to Tilby for the week-end; Ferdy was bringing Lea Makart to hear George play and he particularly wished me to be there. I accepted. Muriel met me at the station.

'How did you find George?' I asked.

'He's very fat, but he seems in great spirits. I think he's pleased to be back again. He's been very sweet to his father.'

'I'm glad of that.'

'Oh, my dear, I do hope Lea Makart will say he's no good. It'll be such a relief to all of us.'

'I'm afraid it'll be a terrible disappointment to him.'

'Life is full of disappointments,' said Muriel crisply. 'But one learns to put up with them.'

I gave her a smile of amusement. We were sitting in a Rolls, and there was a footman as well as a chauffeur on the box. She wore a string of pearls that had probably costs forty thousand pounds. I recollected that in the birthday honours Sir Adolphus Bland had not been one of the three gentlemen on whom the King had been pleased to confer a peerage.

Lea Makart was able to make only a flying visit. She was playing that evening at Brighton and would motor over to Tilby on the Sunday morning for luncheon. She was returning to London the same day because she had a concert in Manchester on the Monday. George was to play in the course of the afternoon.

'He's practising very hard,' his mother told me. 'That's why he didn't come with me to meet you.'

We turned in at the park gates and drove up the imposing avenue of elms that led to the house. I found that there was no party.

I met the dowager Lady Bland for the first time. I had always been curious to see her. I had had in my mind's eye a somewhat sensational picture of an old, old Jewish woman who lived alone in her grand house in Portland Place, and, with a finger in every pie, ruled her family with a despotic hand. She did not disappoint me. She was of commanding presence, rather tall, and stout without being corpulent. Her countenance was markedly Hebraic. She wore a rather heavy moustache and a wig of a peculiarly metallic brown. Her dress was very grand, of black brocade, and she had a row of large diamond stars on her breast and round her neck a chain of diamonds. Diamond rings gleamed on her wrinkled hands. She spoke in a rather harsh voice and with a strong German accent. When I was introduced to her she fixed me with shining eyes. She summed me up with dispatch and to my fancy at all events made no attempt to conceal from me that the judgement she formed was unfavourable.

'You have known my brother Ferdinand for many years, is it not so?' she said, rolling a guttural R. 'My brother Ferdinand has always moved in very good society. Where is Sir Adolphus, Muriel? Does he know your guest is arrived? And will you not send for

George? If he does not know his pieces by now he will not know them by tomorrow.'

Muriel explained that Freddy was finishing a round of golf with his secretary and that she had had George told I was there. Lady Bland looked as though she thought Muriel's replies highly unsatisfactory and turned again to me.

'My daughter-in-law tells me you have been in Italy?'

'Yes, I've only just come back.'

'It is a beautiful country. How is the King?'

I said I did not know.

'I used to know him when he was a little boy. He was not very strong then. His mother, Queen Margherita, was a great friend of mine. They thought he would never marry. The Duchess of Aosta was very angry when he fell in love with the Princess of Montenegro.'

She seemed to belong to some long-past period of history, but she was very alert and I imagine that little escaped her beady eyes. Freddy, very spruce in plus-fours, presently came in. It was amusing and yet a little touching to see this grey-bearded man, as a rule somewhat domineering, so obviously on his best behaviour with the old lady. He called her Mama. Then George came in. He was as fat as ever, but he had taken my advice and had his hair cut; he was losing his boyish looks, but he was a powerful and well-set-up young man. It was good to see the pleasure he took in his tea. He ate quantities of sandwiches and great hunks of cake. He had still a boy's appetite. His father watched him with a tender smile and as I looked at him I could not be surprised at the attachment which they all so obviously felt for him. He had an ingenuousness, a charm, and an enthusiasm which were certainly very pleasant. There was about him a generosity of demeanour, a frankness, and a natural cordiality which could not but make people take to him. I do not know whether it was owing to a hint from his grandmother or merely of his own good nature, but it was plain that he was going out of his way to be nice to his father;

and in his father's soft eyes, in the way he hung upon the boy's words, in his pleased, proud, and happy look, you felt how bitterly the estrangement of the last two years had weighed on him. He adored George.

We played golf in the morning, a three-ball match, since Muriel, having to go to Mass, could not join us, and at one Ferdy arrived in Lea Makart's car. We sat down to luncheon. Of course Lea Makart's reputation was well known to me. She was acknowledged to be the greatest woman pianist in Europe. She was a very old friend of Ferdy's, who with his interest and patronage had greatly helped her at the beginning of her career, and it was he who had arranged for her to come and give her opinion of George's chances. At one time I went as often as I could to hear her play. She had no affectations; she played as a bird sings, without any appearance of effort, very naturally, and the silvery notes dripped from her light fingers in a curiously spontaneous manner, so that it gave you the impression that she was improvising those complicated rhythms. They used to tell me that her technique was wonderful. I could never make up my mind how much the delight of her playing gave me was due to her person. In those days she was the most ethereal thing you could imagine, and it was surprising that a creature so sylphlike should be capable of so much power. She was very slight, pale, with enormous eyes and magnificent black hair, and at the piano she had a childlike wistfulness that was most appealing. She was very beautiful in a hardly human way and when she played, a little smile on her closed lips, she seemed to be remembering things she had heard in another world. Now, however, a woman in her early forties, she was sylphlike no more; she was stout and her face had broadened, she had no longer that lovely remoteness, but the authority of her long succession of triumphs. She was brisk, business-like, and somewhat overwhelming. Her vitality lit her with a natural spotlight as his sanctity surrounds the saint with a halo. She was not interested in anything very much but her own affairs, but since she had humour and knew the world she was able to invest them with gaiety. She held the conversation, but did not absorb it. George talked little. Every now and then she gave him a glance, but did not try to draw him in. I was the only Gentile at the table. All but old Lady Bland spoke perfect English, yet I could not help feeling that they did not speak English like English people; I think they rounded their vowels more than we do, they certainly spoke louder, and the words seemed not to fall, but to gush from their lips. I think that if I had been in another room where I could hear the tone but not the words of their speech I should have thought it was in a foreign language that they were conversing. The effect was slightly disconcerting.

Lea Makart wished to set out for London at about six, so it was arranged that George should play at four. Whatever the result of the audition, I felt that I, a stranger in the circle which her departure must render exclusively domestic, would be in the way and so, pretending an early engagement in town next morning, I asked her if she would take me with her in her car.

At a little before four we all wandered into the drawing-room. Old Lady Bland sat on a sofa with Ferdy; Freddy, Muriel, and I made ourselves comfortable in arm-chairs; and Lea Makart sat by herself. She chose instinctively a high-backed Jacobean chair that had somewhat the air of a throne, and in a yellow dress, with her olive skin, she looked very handsome. She had magnificent eyes. She was very much made up and her mouth was scarlet.

George gave no sign of nervousness. He was already seated at the piano when I went in with his father and mother, and he watched us quietly settling ourselves down. He gave me the shadow of a smile. When he saw that we were all at our ease he began to play. He played Chopin. He played two waltzes that were familiar to me, a polonaise and an etude. He played with a great deal of brio. I wish I knew music well enough to give an exact description of his playing. It had strength, and a youthful exuberance, but I felt that he missed what to me is the peculiar charm of Chopin, the tenderness, the nervous melancholy, the wistful gaiety and the slightly faded romance that reminds me always of an Early Victorian keepsake. And again I had the vague sensation, so slight that it almost escaped me, that the two hands did not quite synchronize. I looked at Ferdy and saw him give his sister a look of faint surprise. Muriel's eyes were fixed on the pianist, but presently she dropped them and for the rest of the time stared at the floor. His father looked at him too, and his eyes were steadfast, but unless I was much mistaken he went pale and his face betrayed something like dismay. Music was in the blood of all of them, all their lives they had heard great pianists in the world, and they judged with instinctive precision. The only person whose face betrayed no emotion was Lea Makart. She listened very attentively. She was as still as an image in a niche.

At last he stopped and turning round on his seat faced her. He did not speak.

'What is it you want me to tell you?' she asked.

They looked into one another's eyes.

'I want you to tell me whether I have any chance of becoming in time a pianist in the first rank.'

'Not in a thousand years.'

For a moment there was dead silence. Freddy's head sank and he looked down at the carpet at his feet. His wife put out her hand and took his. But George continued to look steadily at Lea Makart.

'Ferdy has told me the circumstances,' she said at last. 'Don't think I'm influenced by them. Nothing of this is very important.' She made a sweeping gesture that took in the magnificent room with the beautiful things it contained and all of us. 'If I thought you had in you the makings of an artist I shouldn't hesitate to beseech you to give up everything for art's sake. Art is the only thing that matters. In comparison with art, wealth and rank and power are not worth a straw.' She gave us a look so sincere that it was void of insolence. 'We are the only people who count. We give the world significance. You are only our raw material.'

I was not too pleased to be included with the rest under that heading, but that is neither here nor there.

'Of course I can see that you've worked very hard. Don't think it's been wasted. It will always be a pleasure to you to be able to play the piano and it will enable you to appreciate great playing as no ordinary person can hope to do. Look at your hands. They're not a pianist's hands.'

Involuntarily I glanced at George's hands. I had never noticed them before. I was astounded to see how podgy they were and how short and stumpy the fingers.

'Your ear is not quite perfect. I don't think you can ever hope to be more that a very competent amateur. In art the difference between the amateur and the professional is immeasurable.

George did not reply. Except for his pallor no one would have known that he was listening to the blasting of all his hopes. The silence that fell was quite awful. Lea Makart's eyes suddenly filled with tears.

'But don't take my opinion alone,' she said. 'After all, I'm not infallible. Ask somebody else. You know how good and generous Padereswki is. I'll write to him about you and you can go down and play to him. I'm sure he'll hear you.'

George now gave a little smile. He had very good manners and whatever he was feeling did not want to make the situation too difficult for the others.

'I don't think that's necessary, I am content to accept your verdict. To tell you the truth it's not so very different from my master's in Munich.'

He got up from the piano and lit a cigarette. It eased the strain.

The others moved a little in their chairs. Lea Makart smiled at George.

'Shall I play to you?' she said.

'Yes, do.'

She got up and went to the piano. She took off the rings with which her fingers were laden. She played Bach. I do not know the names of the pieces, but I recognized the still ceremonial of the frenchified little German courts and the sober, thrifty comfort of the burghers, and the dancing on the village green, the green trees that looked like Christmas trees, and the sunlight on the wide German country, and a tender cosiness; and in my nostrils there was a warm scent of the soil and I was conscious of a sturdy strength that seemed to have its roots deep in mother earth, and of an elemental power that was timeless and had no home in space. She played beautifully, with a soft brilliance that made you think of the full moon shining at dusk in the summer sky. With another part of me I watched the others and I saw how intensely they were conscious of the experience. They were rapt. I wished with all my heart that I could get from music the wonderful exaltation that possessed them. She stopped, a smile hovered on her lips, and she put on her rings. George gave a little chuckle.

'That clinches it, I fancy,' he said.

The servants brought in tea and after tea Lea Makart and I bade the company farewell and got into the car. We drove up to London. She talked all the way, if not brilliantly at all events with gusto; she told me of her early years in Manchester and of the struggle of her beginnings. She was very interesting. She never even mentioned George; the episode was of no consequence, it was finished and she thought no more of it.

We little knew what was happening at Tilby. When we left George went out on the terrace and presently his father joined him. Freddy had won the day, but he was not happy. With his more than feminine sensitiveness he felt all that George was feeling, and George's anguish simply broke his heart. He had never loved his son more than then. When he appeared George greeted him with a little smile. Freddy's voice broke. In a sudden and overwhelming emotion he found it in him to surrender the fruits of his victory.

'Look here, old boy,' he said, 'I can't bear to think that you've had such a disappointment. Would you like to go back to Munich for another year and then see?'

George shook his head.

'No, it wouldn't be any good. I've had my chance. Let's call it a day.'

'Try not to take it too hard.'

'You see, the only thing in the world I want is to be a pianist. And there's nothing doing. It's a bit thick if you come to think of it.'

George, trying so hard to be brave, smiled wanly.

'Would you like to go round the world? You can get one of your Oxford pals to go with you and I'll pay all the expenses. You've been working very hard for a long time.'

'Thanks awfully, daddy, we'll talk about it. I'm just going for a stroll now.'

'Shall I come with you?'

'I'd rather go alone.'

Then George did a strange thing. He put his arm round his father's neck, and kissed him on the lips. He gave a funny little moved laugh and walked away. Freddy went back to the drawing-room. His mother, Ferdy, and Muriel were sitting there.

'Freddy, why don't you marry the boy?' said the old lady. 'He is twenty-three. It would take his mind off his troubles and when he is married and has a baby he will soon settle down like everybody else.'

'Whom is he to marry, mamma?' asked Sir Adolphus, smiling.

'That's not so difficult. Lady Frielinghausen came to see me the other day with her daughter Violet. She is a very nice maiden and she will have money of her own. Lady Frielinghausen gave me to understand that her Sir Jacob would come down very handsome if Violet made a good match.'

Muriel flushed.

'I hate Lady Frielinghausen. George is much too young to marry. He can afford to marry anyone he likes.'

Old Lady Bland gave her daughter a strange look.

'You are a very foolish girl, Miriam,' she said, using the name Muriel had long discarded. 'As long as I am here I shall not allow you to commit a foolishness.'

She knew as well as if Muriel had said it in so many words that she wanted George to marry a Gentile, but she knew also that so long as she was alive neither Freddy nor his wife would suggest it.

But George did not go for a walk. Perhaps because the shooting season was about to open he took it into his head to go into the gunroom. He began to clean the gun that his mother had given him on his twentieth birthday. No one had used it since he went to Germany. Suddenly the servants were startled by a report. When they went into the gun-room they found George lying on the floor shot through the heart. Apparently the gun had been loaded and George while playing about with it had accidentally shot himself. One reads of such accidents in the paper often.

THE MUSIC ON THE HILL

"Saki" (H.H. Munro)

SYLVIA SELTOUN ate her breakfast in the morning-room at Yessney with a pleasant sense of ultimate victory, such as a fervent Ironside might have permitted himself on the morrow of Worcester fight. She was scarcely pugnacious by temperament, but belonged to that more successful class of fighters who are pugnacious by circumstance. Fate had willed that her life should be occupied with a series of small struggles, usually with the odds slightly against her, and usually she had just managed to come through winning. And now she felt that she had brought her hardest and certainly her most important struggle to a successful issue. To have married Mortimer Seltoun, "Dead Mortimer" as his more intimate enemies called him, in the teeth of the cold hostility of his family, and in spite of his unaffected indifference to women, was indeed an achievement that had needed some determination and adroitness to carry through; yesterday she had brought her victory to its concluding stage by wrenching her husband away from Town and its group of satellite watering-places and "settling him down," in the vocabulary of her kind, in this remote wood-girt manor farm which was his country house.

"You will never get Mortimer to go," his mother said carpingly, "but if he once goes he'll stay; Yessney throws almost as much a spell over him as Town does. One can understand what holds him to Town, but Yessney ..." and the dowager had shrugged her shoulders.

There was a sombre almost savage wildness about Yessney that was certainly not likely to appeal to town-bred tastes, and Sylvia, notwithstanding her name, was accustomed to nothing much more sylvan than "leafy Kensington." She looked on the country as something excellent and wholesome in its way, which was apt to become troublesome if you encouraged it overmuch. Distrust of town-life had been a new thing with her, born of her marriage with Mortimer, and she had watched with satisfaction the gradual fading of what she called "the Jermyn-street-look" in his eyes as the woods and heather of Yessney had closed in on them yesternight. Her will-power and strategy had prevailed; Mortimer would stay.

Outside the morning-room windows was a triangular slope of turf, which the indulgent might call a lawn, and beyond its low hedge of neglected fuchsia bushes a steeper slope of heather and bracken dropped down into cavernous combes overgrown with oak and yew. In its wild open savagery there seemed a stealthy linking of the joy of life with the terror of unseen things. Sylvia smiled complacently as she gazed with a School-of-Art appreciation at the landscape, and then of a sudden she almost shuddered.

"It is very wild," she said to Mortimer, who had joined her; "one could almost think that in such a place the worship of Pan had never quite died out."

"The worship of Pan has never died out," said Mortimer. "Other newer gods have drawn aside his votaries from time to time, but he is the Nature-God to whom all must come back at last. He has been called the Father of all the Gods, but most of his children have been stillborn."

Sylvia was religious in an honest vaguely devotional kind of way, and did not like to hear her beliefs spoken of as mere aftergrowths, but it was at least something new and hopeful to hear Dead Mortimer speak with such energy and conviction on any subject.

"You don't really believe in Pan?" she asked incredulously.

"I've been a fool in most things," said Mortimer quietly, "but I'm not such a fool as not to believe in Pan when I'm down here. And if you're wise you won't disbelieve in him too boastfully while you're in his country."

It was not till a week later, when Sylvia had exhausted the attractions of the woodland walks round Yessney, that she ventured on a tour of inspection of the farm buildings. A farmyard suggested in her mind a scene of cheerful bustle, with churns and flails and smiling dairymaids, and teams of horses drinking knee-deep in duck-crowded ponds. As she wandered among the gaunt grey buildings of Yessney manor farm her first impression was one of crushing stillness and desolation, as though she had happened on some lone deserted homestead long given over to owl and cobwebs; then came a sense of furtive hostility, the same shadow of unseen things that seemed to lurk in the wooded combes and coppices. From behind heavy doors and shuttered windows came the restless stamp of hoof or rasp of chain halter, and at times a muffled bellow from some stalled beast. From a distant corner a shaggy dog watched her with intent unfriendly eyes; as she drew near it slipped quietly into its kennel, and slipped out again as noiselessly when she had passed by. A few hens, questing for food under a rick, stole away under a gate at her approach. Sylvia felt that if she had come across any human beings in the wilderness of barn and byre they would have fled wraith-like from her gaze. At last, turning a corner quickly, she came upon a living thing that did not fly from her. Astretch in a pool of mud was an enormous sow, gigantic beyond the town-woman's wildest computation of swine-flesh, and speedily alert to resent and if necessary repel the unwonted intrusion. It was Sylvia's turn to make an unobtrusive retreat. As she threaded her way past rickyards and cowsheds and long blank walls, she started suddenly at a strange sound – the echo of a boy's laughter, golden and equivocal. Jan, the only boy employed on the farm, a tow-headed, wizen-faced yokel, was visibly at work on a potato clearing half-way up the nearest hill-side, and Mortimer, when questioned, knew of no other probable or possible begetter of the hidden mockery that had ambushed Sylvia's retreat. The memory of that untraceable echo was added to her other impressions of a furtive sinister "something" that hung around Yessney.

Of Mortimer she saw very little; farm and woods and trout-streams seemed to swallow him up from dawn till dusk. Once, following the direction she had seen him take in the morning, she came to an open space in a nut copse, further shut in by huge yew trees, in the centre of which stood a stone pedestal surmounted by a small bronze figure of a youthful Pan. It was a beautiful piece of workmanship, but her attention was chiefly held by the fact that a newly cut bunch of grapes had been placed as an offering at its feet. Grapes were none too plentiful at the manor house, and Sylvia snatched the bunch angrily from the pedestal. Contemptuous annoyance dominated her thoughts as she strolled homeward, and then gave way to a sharp feeling of something that was very near fright; across a thick tangle of undergrowth a boy's face was scowling at her, brown and beautiful, with unutterably evil eyes. It was a lonely pathway, all pathways around Yessney were lonely for the matter of that, and she sped forward without waiting to give a closer scrutiny to this sudden apparition. It was not until she reached the house that she discovered that she had dropped the bunch of grapes in her flight.

"I saw a youth in the wood to-day," she told Mortimer that evening, "brown-faced and rather handsome, but a scoundrel to look at. A gipsy lad, I suppose."

"A reasonable theory," said Mortimer, "only there aren't any gipsies in these parts at present."

"Then who was he?" asked Sylvia, and as Mortimer appeared to have no theory of his own, she passed on to recount her finding of the votive offering

"I suppose it was your doing," she observed; "it's a harmless piece of lunacy, but people would think you dreadfully silly if they knew of it."

"Did you meddle with it in any way?" asked Mortimer.

"I – I threw the grapes away. It seemed so silly," said Sylvia, watching Mortimer's impassive face for a sign of annoyance.

"I don't think you were wise to do that," he said reflectively. "I've heard it said that the Wood Gods are rather horrible to those who molest them."

"Horrible perhaps to those that believe in them, but you see I don't," retorted Sylvia.

"All the same," said Mortimer in his even, dispassionate tone, "I should avoid the woods and orchards if I were you, and give a wide berth to the horned beasts on the farm."

It was all nonsense, of course, but in that lonely wood-girt spot nonsense seemed able to rear a bastard brood of uneasiness.

"Mortimer," said Sylvia suddenly, "I think we will go back to Town some time soon."

Her victory had not been so complete as she had supposed; it had carried her on to ground that she was already anxious to quit.

"I don't think you will ever go back to Town," said Mortimer. He seemed to be paraphrasing his mother's prediction as to himself.

Sylvia noted with dissatisfaction and some self-contempt that the course of her next afternoon's ramble took her instinctively clear of the network of woods. As to the horned cattle, Mortimer's warning was scarcely needed, for she had always regarded them as of doubtful neutrality at the best: her imagination unsexed the most matronly dairy cows and turned them into bulls liable to "see red" at any moment. The ram who fed in the narrow paddock below the orchards she had adjudged, after ample and cautious probation, to be of docile temper; to-day, however, she decided to leave his docility untested, for the usually tranquil beast was roaming with every sign of restlessness from corner to corner of his meadow. A low, fitful piping, as of some reedy flute, was coming from the depth of a neighbouring copse, and there seemed to be some subtle connection between the animal's restless pacing and the wild music from the wood. Sylvia turned her steps in an upward direction and climbed the heather-clad slopes that stretched in rolling shoulders high above Yessney. She had left the piping notes behind her, but across the wooded combes at her feet the wind brought her another kind of music, the straining bay of hounds in full chase. Yessney was just on the outskirts of the Devon-and-Somerset country, and the hunted deer sometimes came that way. Sylvia could presently see a dark body, breasting hill after hill, and sinking again and again out of sight as he crossed the combes, while behind him steadily swelled that relentless chorus, and she grew tense with the excited sympathy that one feels for any hunted thing in whose capture one is not directly interested. And at last he broke through the outermost line of oak scrub and fern and stood panting in the open, a fat September stag carrying a well-furnished head. His obvious course was to drop down to the brown pools of Undercombe, and thence make his way towards the red deer's favoured sanctuary, the sea. To Sylvia's surprise, however, he turned his head to the upland slope and came lumbering resolutely onward over the heather. "It will be dreadful," she thought, "the hounds will pull him down under my very eyes." But the music of the pack seemed to have died away for a moment, and in its place she heard again that wild piping, which rose now on this side, now on that, as though urging the failing stag to a final effort. Sylvia stood well aside from his path, half hidden in a thick growth of whortle bushes, and watched him swing stiffly upwards, his flanks dark with sweat, the coarse hair on his neck showing light by contrast. The pipe shrilled suddenly around her, and at the same moment the great beast slewed round and bore directly down upon her. In an instant pity for the hunted animal was changed to wild terror at her own danger, the thick heather roots mocked her scrambling effort at flight, and she looked frantically downward for a glimpse of oncoming hounds. The huge antler spikes were within a few yards of her, and in a flash of numbing fear she remembered Mortimer's warning to beware of horned beasts on the farm. And then with a quick throb of joy she saw that she was not alone; a human figure stood a few paces aside, knee-deep in the whortle bushes.

"Drive it off!" she shrieked. But the figure made no answering movement.

The antlers drove straight at her breast, the acrid smell of the hunted animal in her nostrils, but her eyes were filled with the horror of something she saw other than her oncoming death. And in her ears rang the echo of a boy's laugher, golden and equivocal.

THE SECOND SENSE

Nadine Gordimer

The senses 'usually reckoned as five –
sight, hearing, smell, taste, touch.'
Oxford English Dictionary

SHE HAS NEVER FELT any resentment that he became a musician
and she didn't. Could hardly call her amateur flute-playing a
vocation. Envy? Only pride in the achievement that he was born for.
She sits at a computer in a city-government office, earning, under
pleasant enough conditions, a salary that has at least provided
regularly for their basic needs, while his remuneration for the
privilege of being a cellist in a symphony orchestra has been sometimes augmented by chamber-music engagements, sometimes not; in
the summer, the off season for the orchestra, he is dependent on
these performances on the side.

Their social life is in his professional circle – fellow-musicians,
music critics, aficionados whose connections ensure them free tickets,
and the musical families in which most of the orchestra members
grew up, the piano-teacher or choir-singing mothers and church-
organist fathers. When new acquaintances remember to give her the
obligatory polite attention, with the question "What do you do?,"
and she tells them, they clearly wonder what she and the cellist who
is married to her have in common.

As for her, she found when she was still an adolescent – the time
for discovering parental limitations – that her cheerful father, with
his sports shop and the beguiling heartiness that is a qualification for

93

that business, and her mother, with her groupies exchanging talk of female reproductive maladies, from conception to menopause, did not have in their comprehension what it was that she wanted to do. A school outing at sixteen had taken her to a concert where she heard, coming out of a slim tube held to human lips, the call of the flute. Much later, she was able to identify the auditory memory as Mozart's Flute Concerto No. 2 in D, K. 314. Meanwhile, attribution didn't matter any more than the unknown name of a bird that sang heart-piercingly, hidden in her parents' garden. The teacher who had arranged the cultural event was understanding enough to put the girl in touch with a musical youth group in the city. She babysat on weekends to pay for the hire of a flute, and began to attempt to learn how to produce with her own breath and fingers something of what she had heard.

He was among the Youth Players. His instrument was the very antithesis of the flute. Part of the language of early attraction was a kind of repartee about this, showoff, slangy, childish. The sounds he drew from the overgrown violin between his knees: the complaining moo of a sick cow; the rasp of a blunt saw. "Excuse me!" he would say, with a clownish lift of the eyebrows and a down-twisted mouth. His cello, like her flute, was a secondhand donation to the Players from the estate of some old man or woman that was of no interest to family descendants. He tended it in a sensuous way, which, if she had not been so young and innocent, she could have read as an augur of how his lovemaking would begin. Within a year, his exceptional talent had been recognized by the professional musicians who coached these young people voluntarily, and the cello was declared his, no longer on loan.

They played together when alone, to amuse themselves and secretly imagine that they were already in concert performance, the low, powerful cadence coming from the golden-brown body of the cello making her flute voice sound, by contrast, more like that of a squeaking mouse than it would have heard solo. In time, she reached a certain level of minor accomplishment. He couldn't lie to her. They had, with the complicity of his friends, found a place where they could make love – for her, the first time – and, out of commitment to a sincerity beyond their years, he couldn't deceive her and let her suffer the disillusions of persisting with a career that was not open to her level of performance. Already she had been hurt, dismayed at being replaced by other young flautists when ensembles were chosen for public performances by "talented musicians of the future."

"You'll still have the pleasure of playing the instrument you love best."

She would always remember what she said: "The cello is the instrument I love best."

They grew up enough to leave whatever they had been told was home, the parents. They worked as waiters in a restaurant; he gave music lessons in schools. They found a bachelor pad in the run-down part of town, where most whites were afraid to live because blacks had moved there since segregation was outlawed. In the generosity of their passionate happiness they had the expansive impossible need to share something of it – the intangible become tangible – bringing a young man who played pennywhistle *kwela* on the street corner up to their kitchen nook to have a real meal with them, rather than tossing small change into his cap. The white caretaker of the building objected vociferously. "You mad? You mad or what? Inviting blacks to rob and murder you. I can't have it in the building."

She went to computer courses and became proficient. If you're not an artist of some kind, or a doctor, a civil-rights lawyer, what other skill makes you of use in a developing country? Chosen, loved by the one you love – what would be more meaningful than being necessary to him in a practical sense as well, able to support his vocation, his achievements yours by proxy? "What do you do?" "Can't you see? She makes fulfillment possible, for both of them."

Children: married more than a year, they discussed this, the supposedly natural progression in love. Postponed until next time. Next time, they reached the fact: as his unusual gifts began to bring engagements at music festivals abroad and opportunities to play with important – soon-to-be-famous – orchestras, it became clear that he could not be a father, home for the bedtime story every night, or for schoolboy soccer games, at the same time that he was a cellist, soon to have his name on CD labels. If she could get leave from her increasingly responsible job – not too difficult, on occasion – to accompany him, she would not be able to shelve that other responsibility, care of a baby. They made the choice of what they wanted: each other, within a single career. Let her mother and her teatime friends focus on the hazards of reproduction, contemplating their own navels. Let other men seek immortality in progeny; music has no limiting lifespan. An expert told them that the hand-me-down cello was at least seventy years old and the better for it.

One month – when was it? – she found that she was pregnant; kept getting ready to tell him but didn't. He was going on a concert tour in another part of the country, and by the time he came back there was nothing to tell. The process was legal, fortunately, under the new laws of the country, conveniently available at a clinic named for Marie Stopes, a past campaigner for women's rights over their reproductive systems. Better not to have him – what? Even regretful. You know how men, no matter how rewarded with success, buoyant with the tide of applause, still feel they must prove themselves potent. (Where had she picked that up? Eavesdropping, as an adolescent, on tea parties.)

She was so much part of the confraternity of orchestras. The rivalry among the players, drowned out by the exaltation of the music they created together. The gossip – because she was not one of them, both the men and the women trusted her with indiscretions that they wouldn't risk with one another. And when he had differences with guest conductors from Bulgaria or Japan or God knows where, their egos as complex as the pronunciation of their names, his exasperation found relief, as he unburdened himself in bed of the podium dramas and moved on to the haven of love-making. If she was in a low mood – the bungles of an inefficient colleague at work, or her father's "heart condition" and her mother's long complaints over the telephone about his disobeying doctor's orders with his whiskey-swilling golfers – the cello would join them in the bedroom and he'd play for her. Sometimes until she fell asleep to the low tender tones of what had become his voice, to her, the voice of that big curved instrument, its softly buffed surface and graceful bulk held close against his body, sharing the intimacy that was hers. At concerts, when his solo part came, she did not realize that she was smiling in recognition, that this was a voice she would have recognized anywhere, among other cellists bowing other instruments.

Each year, the music critics granted, he played better. Exceeded himself. When distinguished musicians came for the symphony and opera season, it was appropriate that he and she should entertain them at the house, far from the pad they'd once dossed down in. Where others might have kept a special piece of furniture, some inheritance, there stood in the living room, retired, the cello he'd learned to play on loan. He now owned a Guadagnini, a mid-eighteenth-century cello, found for him by a dealer in Prague. He had been hesitant. How could he spend such a fortune? But she was taken aback, indignant, as if someone had already dared to remark on his presumptuous extravagance. "An artist doesn't care for material possessions as such. You're not buying a Mercedes, a yacht!" He had bought a voice of incomparable beauty, somehow human, though of a subtlety and depth – moving from the sonority of an organ to the faintest stir of silences – that no human voice could produce. He admitted – as if telling himself in confidence, as much as her – that this instrument roused in him skilled responses that he hadn't known he had.

In the company of guests whose life was music, as was his, he was as generous as a pop singer responding to fans. He'd bring out the precious presence in its black reliquary, free it, and settle himself to play among the buffet plates and replenished wineglasses. If he'd had a few too many, he'd joke, taking her by the waist for a moment, "I'm just the wunderkind brought in to thump out 'Für Elise' on the piano," and then he'd play so purely that the voice of the aristocratic cello, which she knew as well as she had that of the charity one, made all social exchange strangely trivial. But the musicians, entre-preneurs, and guests favored to be among them applauded, descended upon him, the husbands and gay men hunching his shoulders in their grasp, the women giving accolades, sometimes landing on his lips. It wasn't unusual for one of the distinguished male guests – not the Japanese but especially the elderly German or Italian conductors – to make a pass at her. She knew that she was attractive enough, intelligent enough, musically and otherwise (even her buffet was good), for this to happen, but she was aware that it was really the bloom of being the outstandingly gifted cellist's woman that motivated these advances. Imagine if the next time the celebrated cellist played under your baton in Strasbourg you were able to remark to another musician your own age, "And his wife's pretty good, too, in bed."

Once the guests had gone, host and hostess laughed about the flirtatious attention, which he hadn't failed to notice. The cello stood grandly against the wall in the bedroom. Burglaries were common in the suburbs, and there were knowledgeable gangs who looked not for TV sets and computers but for paintings and other valuable objects. Anyone who broke in would have to come into the bedroom to catch sight of the noble Guadagnini, and face the revolver kept under the pillow.

Bach, Mozart, Hindemith, Cage, Stockhausen, and Glass were no longer regarded in the performance world patronizingly as music that blacks neither enjoyed nor understood. The national orchestra, which was his base – while his prestige meant that he could absent himself whenever he was invited to festivals or to join a string ensemble on tour – had a black trombonist and a young second violinist with African braids that fell about her ebony neck as she wielded her bow. She spoke German to a visiting Austrian conductor; she'd had a scholarship to study in Strasbourg. Professional musicians have always been a league of nations; for a time, the orchestra had a tympanist from Brazil. He became a special friend, and on occasion a live-in guest, who kept her company when the beautiful cello accompanied its player overseas.

She was aware that, without a particular ability of her own, beyond an everyday competence in commercial communications, she was privileged enough to have an interesting life, and a remarkably talented man whose milieu was also hers.

What was the phrase? She "saw the world," often travelling with him. She had arranged a leave, to accompany the string ensemble to Berlin, for one of the many musical events in commemoration of the two-hundred-and-fiftieth anniversary of Mozart's birth, but then couldn't go after all, because her father was dying – cheerfully, but her mother had to be supported.

The ensemble met with exceptional success, among musicians of high reputation from many countries. He brought back a folder full of press cuttings – a few in English – glowing. He tipped his head dismissively – perhaps you can become inured to praise, in time, or perhaps he was tired, drained by the demands of his music. She had suggestions for relaxation: a film, a dinner, away from concert-hall discipline, with the ensemble musicians; one becomes close to people – a special relationship that she had long recognized in him – with whom one has achieved something. He was not enthusiastic. "Next week, next week." He took the revered cello out of its solitude in the case carved to its shape and played, to himself, to her – well, she was in the room those evenings.

It is his voice, that glorious voice of his cello, saying something different, speaking not to her but to some other.

He makes love to her. Isn't that always the signal of return after he has been away?

There's a deliberation in the caresses. She is almost moved to say stupidly what they've never thought to say to each other: Do you still love me?

He begins to absent himself from her at unexplained times or for obligations that he must know she knows don't exist.

The voice of the cello doesn't lie.

How to apply to the life of this man that shabby ordinary circumstance – what's the phrase? He's *having an affair*. Artists of any kind attract women. They sniff out some mysterious energy of devotion there, which will always be the rival of their own usually reliable powers of seduction. Something that will be kept from even the most desired woman. Who could know that attraction better than she? But, for her, that other, mysterious energy of devotion has now made of love a threesome.

The cello with its curved body reverentially in the bedroom.

What woman?

At music festivals around the world, the same orchestral players, the same quartets and trios keep meeting. In different countries, they share a map of common experience, live in the same hotels, exchange discoveries of restaurants, complaints about concert-hall acoustics, and enthusiasm over audience response. If it were some musician encountered on a particular tour, that didn't necessarily mean that the affair was a brief one, which had ended when the man and the woman went their separate ways, seas and continents apart; they might meet again, plan to, at the next festival, somewhere else in the world – Vienna, Jerusalem, Sydney – where he had played or was contracted to play soon. The stimulation not only of performance before an unknown audience but of meeting again, the excitement of being presented with the opportunity to continue something interrupted.

Or was the woman nearer home? A member of the national orchestra in which he and his cello were star performers? That was an identification she found hard to look for, considering their company of friends in this way. A young woman, of course, a younger woman than herself. But wasn't that just the inevitable decided at her mother's tea-table forum? The clarinet player was in her late forties, endowed with fine breasts in décolleté and a delightful wit. There was often repartee between them, the clarinet and the cello, over drinks. The pianist, young with waist-length red-out-of-the-bottle hair, was a lesbian kept under strict guard by her woman. The third and last female musician in the orchestra was also the last whom one would be crass enough to think of: her name was Khomotso; she was the second violinist of extraordinary talent, one of the two black musicians. She was so young; she had given birth to an adored baby, who, for the first few months of life, had been brought to rehearsals in the car of Khomotso's sister so that the mother could suckle the infant there. The director of the orchestra gave an interview to a Sunday newspaper about this, as an example of the orchestra's adaptation to the human values of the new South Africa. The violinist was certainly the prettiest, the most desirable, of the women in whose company the cellist spent the intense part of his days and nights, but respect, *his* human feeling, would be stronger than sexual attraction, his identification with her as a musician would make distracting her from that taboo. As for him, wouldn't it look like the old South Africa – a white man "taking advantage of" the precariously balanced life of a young black woman?

His lover might also have been one of the faithful season-ticket holders who gave post-performance parties. He had a lunchtime friendship with one of the male regulars, an industrialist and amateur viola player with a fine music library, from which he was free to borrow. Or it might have been the wife of one of these men. Many of the wives were themselves career women, much younger than their wealthy husbands, bringing intelligence of a commitment to ideas and activities outside the arts, as well as what he might see as sexual availability.

It was no longer assumed that she would go with him, as she always had, when he accepted invitations to receptions or private houses; the unspoken implication was that these were now strictly professional. He no longer suggested what had also been assumed – that when he was to give a recital in another city in their home country she would, of course, be there. He packed his overnight bag on their bed, took up the black-clad body of the cello, and kissed her goodbye. There were well-spaced acts of dutiful intercourse, as if it were as routine as a regular haircut. She began to want to avoid the approach in bed, and then grew fearful that she would send him to the other woman by suggesting that she did not desire him; at the same time, she wanted terribly to put her hands, her mouth on the body beside her, no matter the humiliation of the act, which he fulfilled like a medical procedure, prescribed to satisfy her. A bill to be paid.

She waited for him to speak. About what had happened. To trust the long confidence between them. He never did. She did not ask, because she was also afraid that what had happened, once admitted, would be irrevocably real.

One night, he got up in the dark, took the cello out of its bed, and played. She woke to the voice, saying something passionately angry in its deepest bass.

Then there came the time when – was it possible, in his magnificent, exquisite playing? – there was a disharmony, the low notes dragging as if the cello were refusing him. Nights, weeks, the same.

So. She knew that the affair was over. She felt a pull of sadness –
for him. For herself, nothing. By never confronting him she had
stunned herself.

Soon he came to her again. The three of them – he, she, and the
cello against the wall – were together.

He made love better than ever remembered, caresses not known,
more subtle, more anticipatory of what could be roused in her, what
she was capable of feeling, needing. As if he'd had the experience of
a different instrument to learn from.

EDWARD THE CONQUEROR

Roald Dahl

LOUISA, HOLDING A DISHCLOTH in her hand, stepped out of the kitchen door at the back of the house into the cool October sunshine.

'Edward!' she called. '*Ed-ward!* Lunch is ready!'

She paused a moment, listening; then she strolled out on to the lawn and continued across it – a little shadow attending her – skirting the rose bed and touching the sundial lightly with one finger as she went by. She moved rather gracefully for a woman who was small and plump, with a lilt in her walk and a gentle swinging of the shoulders and the arms. She passed under the mulberry tree on to the brick path, then went all the way along the path until she came to the place where she could look down into the dip at the end of this large garden.

'*Edward!* Lunch'

She could see him now, about eighty yards away, down in the dip on the edge of the wood – the tallish narrow figure in Khaki slacks and dark green sweater, working beside a big bonfire with a fork in his hands, pitching brambles on to the top of the fire. It was blazing fiercely, with orange flames and clouds of milky smoke, and the smoke was drifting back over the garden with a wonderful scent of autumn and burning leaves.

Louisa went down the slope towards her husband. Had she wanted, she could easily have called again and made herself heard, but there was something about a first-class bonfire that impelled her towards it, right up close so she could feel the heat and listen to it burn.

Portrait of Hungarian pianist and composer Franz Liszt (1811-1886) by Henri Lehmann (1814-1882), 1839. Musée Carnavalet, Paris. Oil on canvas.

'Lunch,' she said, approaching.

'Oh, hello. All right – yes. I'm coming.'

'*What* a good fire.'

'I've decided to clear this place right out,' her husband said. 'I'm sick and tired of all these brambles.' His long face was wet with perspiration. There were small beads of it clinging all over his moustache like dew, and two little rivers were running down his throat on to the turtleneck of the sweater.

'You better be careful you don't overdo it, Edward.'

'Louisa, I do wish you'd stop treating me as though I were eighty. A bit of exercise never did anyone any harm.'

'Yes dear, I know. Oh, Edward! Look! Look!'

The man turned and looked at Louisa, who was pointing now to the far side of the bonfire.

'Look, Edward! The cat!'

Sitting on the ground, so close to the fire that the flames sometimes seemed actually to be touching it, was a large cat of a most unusual colour. It stayed quite still, with its head on one side and its nose in the air, watching the man and the woman with a cool yellow eye.

'It'll get burnt!' Louisa cried, and she dropped the dishcloth and darted swiftly in and grabbed it with both hands, whisking it away and putting in on the grass well clear of the flames.

'You crazy cat,' she said, dusting off her hands. 'What's the matter with you?'

'Cats know what they're doing,' the husband said. 'You'll never find a cat doing something it doesn't want. Not cats.'

'Whose is it? You ever seen it before?'

'No, I never have. Damn peculiar colour.'

The cat had seated itself on the grass and was regarding them with a sidewise look. There was a veiled inward expression about the eyes, something curiously omniscient and pensive, and around the nose a most delicate air of contempt, as though the sight of these two middle-aged persons – the one small, plump, and rosy, the other lean and extremely sweaty – were a matter of some surprise but very little importance. For a cat, it certainly had an unusual colour – a pure silvery grey with no blue in it at all – and the hair was very long and silky.

Louisa bent down and stroked its head. 'You must go home,' she said. 'Be a good cat now and go on home to where you belong.'

The man and wife started to stroll back up the hill towards the house. The cat got up and followed, at a distance first, but edging closer and closer as they went along. Soon it was alongside them, then it was ahead, leading the way across the lawn to the house, walking as though it owned the whole place, holding its tail straight up in the air, like a mast.

'Go home,' the man said. 'Go on home. We don't want you.'

But when they reached the house, it came in with them, and Louisa gave it some milk in the kitchen. During lunch, it hopped up on to the spare chair between them and sat through the meal with its head just above the level of the table watching the proceedings with those dark-yellow eyes which kept moving slowly from the woman to the man and back again.

'I don't like this cat,' Edward said.

'Oh, I think it's a beautiful cat. I hope it stays a little while.'

'Now, listen to me, Louisa. The creature can't possibly stay here. It belongs to someone else. It's lost. And if it's still trying to hang around this afternoon, you'd better take it to the police. They'll see it gets home.'

After lunch, Edward returned to his gardening. Louisa, as usual, went to the piano. She was a competent pianist and a genuine music-lover, and almost every afternoon she spent an hour or so playing for herself. The cat was now lying on the sofa, and she paused to stroke it as she went by. It opened its eyes, looked at her for a moment, then closed them again and went back to sleep.

'You're an awfully nice cat,' she said. 'And such a beautiful colour. I wish I could keep you.' Then her fingers, moving over the fur on the cat's head, came into contact with a small lump, a little growth just above the right eye.

'Poor cat,' she said. 'You've got bumps on your beautiful face. You must be getting old.'

She went over and sat down on the long piano stool but she didn't immediately start to play. One of her special little pleasures was to make every day a kind of concert day, with a carefully arranged programme which she worked out in detail before she began. She never liked to break her enjoyment by having to stop while she wondered what to play next. All she wanted was a brief pause after each piece while the audience clapped enthusiastically and called for more. It was so much nicer to imagine an audience and now and again while she was playing – on the lucky days, that is – the room would begin to swim and fade and darken, and she would see nothing but row upon row of seats and a sea of white faces upturned towards her, listening with a rapt and adoring concentration.

Sometimes she played from memory, sometimes from music. Today she would play from memory; that was the way she felt. And what should the programme be? She sat before the piano with her small hands clasped on her lap, a plump rosy little person with a round and still quite pretty face, her hair done up in a neat bun at the back of her head. By looking slightly to the right, she could see the cat curled up asleep on the sofa, and its silvery grey coat was beautiful against the purple of the cushion. How about some Bach to begin with? Or, better still, Vivaldi. The Bach adaptation for organ of the D minor Concerto Grosso. Yes, that first. Then perhaps a little Schumann. *Carnaval*? That would be fun. And after that – well, a touch of Liszt for a change. One of the *Petrarch Sonnets*. The second one – that was the loveliest – The E major. Then another Schumann, another of his gay ones – *Kinderscenen*. And lastly, for the encore, a Brahms waltz, or maybe two of them if she felt like it.

Vivaldi, Schumann, Liszt, Schumann, Brahms. A very nice programme, one that she could play easily without the music. She moved herself a little closer to the piano and paused a moment while someone in the audience – already she could feel that this was one of the lucky days – while someone in the audience had his last cough; then, with the slow grace that accompanied nearly all her movements, she lifted her hands to the keyboard and began to play.

She wasn't, at that particular moment, watching the cat – as a matter of fact she had forgotten its presence – but as the first deep notes of the Vivaldi sounded softly in the room, she became aware, out of the corner of one eye, of a sudden flurry, a flash of movement on the sofa to her right. She stopped playing at once. 'What is it?' she said, turning to the cat. 'What's the matter?'

The animal, who a few seconds before had been sleeping peacefully, was now sitting bolt upright on the sofa, very tense, the whole body acquiver, ears up and eyes wide open, staring at the piano.

'Did I frighten you?' she asked gently. 'Perhaps you've never heard music before.'

No, she told herself. I don't think that's what it is. On second thoughts, it seemed to her that the cat's attitude was not one of fear. There was no shrinking or backing away. If anything, there was a leaning forward, a kind of eagerness about the creature, and the face – well, there was rather an odd expression on the face, something of a mixture between surprise and shock. Of course, the face of a cat is a small and fairly expressionless thing, but if you watch carefully the eyes and ears working together, and particularly that little area of mobile skin below the ears and slightly to one side, you can occasionally see the reflection of very powerful emotions. Louisa was watching the face closely now, and because she was curious to see what would happen a second time, she reached out her hands to keyboard and began again to play the Vivaldi.

This time the cat was ready for it, and all that happened to begin with was a small extra tensing of the body. But as the music swelled and quickened into that first exciting rhythm of the introduction to the fugue, a strange look that amounted almost to ecstasy began to settle upon the creature's face. The ears, which up to then had been pricked up straight, were gradually drawn back, the eyelids drooped, the head went over to one side, and at that moment Louisa could have sworn that the animal was actually *appreciating* the work.

What she saw (or thought she saw) was something she had noticed many times on the faces of people listening very closely to a piece of music. When the sound takes complete hold of them and drowns them in itself, a peculiar, intensely ecstatic look comes over them that you can recognize as easily as a smile. So far as Louisa could see, the cat was now wearing almost exactly this kind of look.

Louisa finished the fugue, then played the siciliana, and all the way through she kept watching the cat on the sofa. The final proof for her that the animal was listening came at the end, when the music stopped. It blinked, stirred itself a little, stretched a leg, settled in a more comfortable position, took a quick glance round the room, then looked expectantly in her direction. It was precisely the way a concert-goer reacts when the music momentarily releases him in the pause between two movements of a symphony. The behaviour was so thoroughly human it gave her a queer, agitated feeling in the chest.

'You like that?' she asked. 'You like Vivaldi?'

The moment she'd spoken, she felt ridiculous, but not – and this to her was a trifle sinister – not quite so ridiculous as she knew she should have felt.

Well, there was nothing for it now except to go straight ahead with the next number on the programme, which was *Carnaval*. As soon as she began to play, the cat again stiffened and sat up straighter; then, as it became slowly and blissfully saturated with the sound, it relapsed into that queer melting mood of ecstasy that seemed to have something to do with drowning and with dreaming. It was really an extravagant sight – quite a comical one, too – to see this silvery cat sitting on the sofa and being carried away like this. And what made it more screwy than ever, Louisa thought, was the fact that this music, which the animal seemed to be enjoying so much, was manifestly too *difficult*, too *classical*, to be appreciated by the majority of humans in the world.

Maybe, she thought, the creature's not really enjoying it at all. Maybe it's a sort of hypnotic reaction, like with snakes. After all, if you can charm a snake with music, then why not a cat? Except that millions of cats hear the stuff every day of their lives, on radio and gramophone and piano, and, as far as she knew, there'd never yet been a case of one behaving like this. This one was acting as though it were following every single note. It was certainly a fantastic thing.

But was it not also a wonderful thing? Indeed it was. In fact, unless she was much mistaken, it was a kind of miracle, one of those animal miracles that happen about once every hundred years.

'I could see you *loved* that one,' she said when the piece was over. 'Although I'm sorry I didn't play it any too well today. Which did you like best – the Vivaldi or the Schumann?'

The cat made no reply, so Louisa, fearing she might lose the attention of her listener, went straight into the next part of the programme – Liszt's second *Petrarch Sonnet*.

And now an extraordinary thing happened. She hadn't played more than three or four bars when the animal's whiskers began perceptibly to twitch. Slowly it drew itself up to an extra height, laid its head on one side, then on the other, and stared into space with a kind of frowning concentrated look that seemed to say, 'What's this? Don't tell me. I know it so well, but just for the moment I don't seem able to place it.' Louisa was fascinated, and with her little mouth half open and half smiling, she continued to play, waiting to see what on earth was going to happen next.

The cat stood up, walked to one end of the sofa, sat down again, listened some more; then all at once it bounded to the floor and leaped up on to the piano stool beside her. There it sat, listening intently to the lovely sonnet, not dreamily this time, but very erect, the large yellow eyes fixed upon Louisa's fingers.

'Well!' she said as she struck the last chord. 'So you came up to sit beside me did you? You like this better than the sofa? All right, I'll let you stay, but you must keep still and not jump about.' She put out a hand and stroked the cat softly along the back, from head to tail. 'That was Liszt,' she went on. 'Mind you, he can sometimes be quite horribly vulgar, but in things like this he's really charming.'

She was beginning to enjoy this odd animal pantomime, so she went straight on into the next item on the programme, Schumann's *Kinderscenen*.

She hadn't been playing for more than a minute or two when she realized that the cat had moved again, and was now back in its old place on the sofa. She'd been watching her hands at the time, and presumably that was why she hadn't even noticed its going; all the same, it must have been an extremely swift and silent move. The cat was still staring at her, still apparently attending closely to the music, and yet it seemed to Louisa that there was not now the same rapturous enthusiasm there'd been during the previous piece, the Liszt. In addition, the act of leaving the stool and return-ing to the sofa appeared in itself to be a mild but positive gesture of disappointment.

'What's the matter?' she asked when it was over. 'What's wrong with Schumann? What's so marvellous about Liszt?' The cat looked straight back at her with those yellow eyes that had small jet-black bars lying vertically in their centres.

This, she told herself, is really beginning to get interesting – a trifle spooky, too, when she came to think of it. But one look at the cat sitting there on the sofa, so bright and attentive, so obviously waiting for more music, quickly reassured her.

'All right,' she said. 'I'll tell you what I'm going to do. I'm going to alter my programme specially for you. You seem to like Liszt so much, I'll give you another.'

She hesitated, searching her memory for a good Liszt; then softly she began to play one of the twelve little pieces from *Der Weihnachtsbaum*. She was now watching the cat very closely, and the first thing she noticed was that the whiskers again began to twitch. It jumped down to the carpet, stood still a moment, inclining its head, quivering with excitement, and then, with a slow, silky stride, it walked around the piano, hopped up on the stool, and sat down beside her.

They were in the middle of all this when Edward came in from the garden.

'Edward!' Louisa cried, jumping up. 'Oh, Edward, darling! Listen to this! Listen what's happened!'

'What is it now?' he said. 'I'd like some tea.' He had one of those narrow, sharp-nosed, faintly magenta faces, and the sweat was making it shine as though it were a long wet grape.

'It's the cat!' Louisa cried, pointing to it sitting quietly on the piano stool. 'Just *wait* till you hear what's happened!'

'I thought I told you to take it to the police.'

'But, Edward, *listen* to me. This is *terribly* exciting. This is a *musical* cat.'

'Oh, yes?'

'This cat can appreciate music, and it can understand it too.'

'Now stop this nonsense, Louisa, and for God's sake let's have some tea. I'm hot and tired from cutting brambles and building bonfires.' He sat down in an armchair, took a cigarette from a box beside him, and lit it with an immense patent lighter that stood near the box.

'What you don't understand,' said Louisa, 'is that something extremely exciting has been happening here in our own house while you were out, something that may even be … well … almost momentous.'

'I'm quite sure of that.'

'Edward, *please!*'

Louisa was standing by the piano, her little pink face pinker than ever, a scarlet rose high up on each cheek. 'If you want to know,' she said, 'I'll tell you what I think.'

'I'm listening, dear.'

'I think it might be possible that we are at this moment sitting in the presence of –' She stopped, as though suddenly sensing the absurdity of the thought.

'Yes?'

'You may think it silly, Edward, but it's honestly what I think.'

'In the presence of whom, for heaven's sake?'

'Of Franz Liszt himself!'

Her husband took a long slow pull at his cigarette and blew the smoke up at the ceiling. He had the tight-skinned concave cheeks of a man who has worn a full set of dentures for many years, and every time he sucked at a cigarette, the cheeks went in even more, and the bones of his face stood out like a skeleton's. 'I don't get you,' he said.

'Edward, listen to me. From what I've seen this afternoon with my own eyes, it really looks as though this might be some sort of reincarnation.'

'You mean this lousy cat?'

'Don't talk like that, dear, please.'

'You're not ill, are you, Louisa?'

'I'm perfectly all right, thank you very much. I'm a bit confused – I don't mind admitting it, but who wouldn't be after what's just happened? Edward, I swear to you –'

'What *did* happen, if I may ask?'

Louisa told him, and all the while she was speaking, her husband lay sprawled in the chair with his legs stretched out in front of him, sucking at his cigarette and blowing the smoke up at the ceiling. There was a thin cynical smile on his mouth.

'I don't see anything very unusual about that,' he said when it was over. 'All it is – it's a trick cat. It's been taught tricks, that's all.'

'Don't be so silly, Edward. Every time I play Liszt, he gets all excited and comes running over to sit on the stool beside me. But only for Liszt, and nobody can teach a cat the difference between Liszt and Schumann. You don't even know it yourself. But this one can do it every single time. Quite obscure Liszt, too.'

'Twice,' the husband said. 'He's only done it twice.'

'Twice is enough.'

'Let's see him do it again. Come on.'

'No,' Louisa said. 'Definitely not. Because if this *is* Liszt, as I believe it is, or anyway the soul of Liszt or whatever it is that comes back, then it's certainly not right or even very kind to put him through a lot of silly undignified tests.'

'My dear woman! This is a *cat* – a rather stupid grey cat that nearly got its coat singed by the bonfire this morning in the garden. And anyway, what do you know about reincarnation?'

'If the soul is there, that's enough for me,' Louisa said firmly. 'That's all that counts.'

'Come on, then. Let's see him perform. Let's see him tell the difference between his own stuff and someone else's.'

'No, Edward. I've told you before, I refuse to put him through any more silly circus tests. He's had quite enough of that for one day. But

I'll tell you what I *will* do. I'll play him a little more of his own music.'

'A fat lot that'll prove.'

'You watch. And one thing is certain – as soon as he recognizes it, he'll refuse to budge off that stool where he's sitting now.'

Louisa went to the music shelf, took down a book of Liszt, thumbed through it quickly, and chose another of his finer compositions – the B minor Sonata. She had meant to play only the first part of the work, but once she got started and saw how the cat was sitting there literally quivering with pleasure and watching her hands with that rapturous concentrated look, she didn't have the heart to stop. She played it all the way through. When it was finished, she glanced up at her husband and smiled. 'There you see,' she said. 'You can't tell me he wasn't absolutely *loving* it.'

'He just likes the noise, that's all.'

'He was *loving* it. Weren't you, darling?' she said, lifting the cat in her arms. 'Oh, my goodness, if only he could talk. Just think of it, dear – he met Beethoven in his youth! He knew Schubert and Mendelssohn and Schumann and Berlioz and Grieg and Delacroix and Ingres and Heine and Balzac. And let me see … My heavens, he was Wagner's father-in-law! I'm holding Wagner's father-in-law in my arms!'

'Louisa!' her husband said sharply, sitting up straight. 'Pull yourself together.' There was a new edge to his voice now, and he spoke louder.

Louisa glanced up quickly. 'Edward, I do believe you're jealous!'

'Of a miserable grey cat!'

'Then don't be so grumpy and cynical about it all. If you're going to behave like this, the best thing you can do is to go back to your gardening and leave the two of us together in peace. That will be best for all of us, won't it, darling?' she said, addressing the cat, stroking its head. 'And later on this evening, we shall have some more

An ageing Franz Liszt, 1884 by Franz von Lenbach (1836-1904).

music together, you and I, some more of your own work. Oh, yes,' she said, kissing the creature several times on the neck, 'and we might have a little Chopin, too. You needn't tell me – I happen to know you adore Chopin. You used to be great friends with him, didn't you, darling. As a matter of fact – if I remember rightly – it was in Chopin's apartment that you met the great love of your life, Madame Something-or-Other. Had three illegitimate children by her, too, didn't you? Yes, you did, you naughty thing, and don't go trying to deny it. So you shall have some Chopin, she said, kissing the cat again, 'and that'll probably bring back all sorts of lovely memories to you, won't it?'

'Louisa, stop this at once!'

'Oh, don't be so stuffy, Edward.'

'You're behaving like a perfect idiot, woman. And anyway, you forget we're going out this evening, to Bill and Betty's for canasta.

'Oh, but I couldn't *possibly* go out now. There's no question of that.

Edward got up slowly from his chair, then bent down and stubbed his cigarette hard into the ash-tray. 'Tell me something,' he said quietly. 'You don't really believe this – this twaddle you're talking, do you?'

'But of course I do. I don't think there's any question about it now. And, what's more, I consider that it puts a tremendous responsibility upon us, Edward – upon both of us. You as well.

'You know what I think,' he said. 'I think you ought to see a doctor. And damn quick, too.'

With that, he turned and stalked out of the room, through the French windows, back into the garden.

Louisa watched him striding across the lawn towards his bonfire and his brambles, and she waited until he was out of sight before she turned and ran to the front door, still carrying the cat.

Soon she was in the car, driving to town.

She parked in front of the library, locked the cat in the car, hurried up the steps into the building, and headed straight for the reference room. There she began searching the cards for books on two subjects – REINCARNATION and LISZT.

Under REINCARNATION she found something called *Recurring Earth-Lives – How and Why*, by a man called F. Milton Willis, published in 1921. Under LISZT she found two biographical volumes. She took out all three books, returned to the car, and drove home.

Back in the house, she placed the cat on the sofa, sat herself down beside it with her books, and prepared to do some serious reading. She would begin, she decided, with Mr F. Milton Willis's work. The volume was thin and a trifle soiled, but it had a good heavy feel to it, and the author's name had an authoritative ring.

The doctrine of reincarnation, she read, states that spiritual souls pass from higher to higher forms of animals. 'A man can, for instance, no more be reborn as an animal than an adult can re-become a child.'

She read this again. But how did he know? How could he be so sure? He couldn't. No one could possibly be certain about a thing like that. At the same time, the statement took a good deal of the wind out of her sails.

'Around the centre of consciousness of each of us, there are, besides the dense outer body, four other bodies, invisible to the eye of flesh, but perfectly visible to people whose faculties of perception of superphysical things have undergone the requisite development ...'

She didn't understand that one at all, but she read on, and soon she came to an interesting passage that told how long a soul usually stayed away from the earth before returning in someone else's body. The time varied according to type, and Mr Willis gave the following breakdown:

Drunkards and the unemployable	40/50	YEARS
Unskilled labourers	60/100	"
Skilled workers	100/200	"
The *bourgeoisie*	200/300	"
The upper-middle classes	500	"
The highest class of gentleman farmers	600/1,000	"
Those in the Path of Initiation	1,500/2,000	"

Quickly she referred to one of the other books, to find out how long Liszt had been dead. It said he died in Bayreuth in 1886. That was sixty-seven years ago. Therefore, according to Mr Willis, he'd have to have been an unskilled labourer to come back so soon. That didn't seem to fit at all. On the other hand, she didn't think much of the author's methods of grading. According to him, 'the highest class of gentleman farmer' was just about the most superior being on the earth. Red jackets and stirrup cups and the bloody, sadistic murder of the fox. No, she thought, that isn't right. It was a pleasure to find herself beginning to doubt Mr Willis.

Later in the book, she came upon a list of some of the more famous reincarnations. Epicteus, she was told, returned to earth as Ralph Waldo Emerson. Cicero came back as Gladstone, Alfred the Great as Queen Victoria, William the Conqueror as Lord Kitchener. Ashoka Vardhana, King of India in 272 B.C. came back as Colonel Henry Steel Olcott, an esteemed American lawyer. Pythagoras returned as Master Koot Hoomi, the gentleman who found the Theosophical Society with Mme Blavatsky and Colonel H.S. Olcott (the esteemed American lawyer, alias Ashoka Vardhana, King of India). It didn't say who Mme Blavatsky had been. 'But Theodore Roosevelt,' it said, 'has for numbers of incarnations played great parts as a leader of men ... From him descended the royal line of ancient Chaldea, he having been, about 30,000 B.C., appointed Governor of Chaldea by the Ego we know as Caesar who was then ruler of Persia ... Roosevelt and Caesar have been together time after time as military and administrative leaders; at one time, many thousands of years ago, they were husband and wife ...'

That was enough for Louisa. Mr F. Milton Willis was clearly nothing but a guesser. She was not impressed by his dogmatic assertions. The fellow was probably on the right track, but his pronouncements were extravagant, especially the first one of all, about animals. Soon she hoped to be able to confound the whole Theosophical Society with her proof that man could indeed reappear as a lower animal. Also that he did not have to be an unskilled labourer to come back within a hundred years.

She now turned to one of the Liszt biographies and she was glancing through it casually when her husband came in again from the garden.

'What are you doing now?' he asked.

'Oh – just checking up a little here and there. Listen, my dear, did you know that Theodore Roosevelt once was Caesar's wife?'

'Louisa,' he said, 'look – why don't we stop this nonsense? I don't like to see you making a fool of yourself like this. Just give me that goddamn cat and I'll take it to the police station myself.'

Louisa didn't seem to hear him. She was staring open-mouthed at a picture of Liszt in the book that lay on her lap. 'My God!' she cried. 'Edward, look!'

'What?'

'Look! The warts on his face! I forgot all about them! He had these great warts on his face and it was a famous thing. Even his students used to cultivate little tufts of hair on their own faces in the same spots, just to be like him.'

'What's that got to do with it?'

'Nothing, I mean not the students. But the warts have.

'Oh, Christ,' the man said. 'Oh, Christ God Almighty.'

'The cat has them, too! Look. I'll show you.'

She took the animal on her lap and began examining its face. 'There! There's one! And there's another! Wait a minute! I do believe they're in the same places! Where's that picture?'

It was a famous portrait of the musician in his old age, showing the fine powerful face framed in a mass of long grey hair that covered his ears and came half-way down his neck. On the face itself, each large wart had been faithfully reproduced, and there were five of them in all.

'Now, in the picture there's *one* above the right eyebrow.' She looked above the right eyebrow of the cat. 'Yes! It's there! In exactly the same place! And another on the left, at the top of the nose. That one's there, too! And one just below it on the cheek. And two fairly close together under the chin on the right side. Edward! Edward! Come and look! They're exactly the same.'

'It doesn't prove a thing.'

She looked up at her husband who was standing in the centre of the room in his green sweater and khaki slacks, still perspiring freely. 'You're scared, aren't you, Edward? Scared of losing your precious dignity and having people think you might be making a fool of yourself just for once.'

'I refuse to get hysterical about it, that's all.'

Louisa turned back to the book and began reading some more. 'This is interesting,' she said. It says here that Liszt loved all of Chopin's work except one – the Scherzo in B flat minor. Apparently he hated that. He called it the "Governess Scherzo", and said that it ought to be reserved solely for people in that profession.

'So what?'

'Edward, listen. As you insist on being so horrid about all this, I'll tell you what I'm going to do. I'm going to play this scherzo right now and you can stay here and see what happens.'

'And then maybe you will deign to get us some supper.'

Louisa got up and took from the shelf a large green volume containing all of Chopin's works. 'Here it is. Oh yes, I remember it. It *is* rather awful. Now, listen – or, rather, watch. Watch to see what he does.'

She placed the music on the piano and sat down. Her husband remained standing. He had his hands in his pockets and a cigarette in his mouth, and in spite of himself he was watching the cat, which was now dozing on the sofa. When Louisa began to play, the first effect was as dramatic as ever. The animal jumped up as though it had been stung, and it stood motionless for at least a minute, the ears pricked up, the whole body quivering. Then it became restless and began to walk back and forth along the length of the sofa. Finally, it hopped down on to the floor, and with its nose and tail held high in the air, it marched slowly, majestically, from the room.

'There!' Louisa cried, jumping up and running after it. 'That does it! That really proves it!' She came back carrying the cat which she put down again on the sofa. Her whole face was shining with excitement now, her fists were clenched white, and the little bun on top of her head was loosening and going over to one side. 'What about it, Edward? What d'you think?' She was laughing nervously as she spoke.

'I must say it was quite amusing.'

'*Amusing!* My dear Edward, it's the most wonderful thing that's ever happened! Oh, goodness me!' she cried, picking up the cat again and hugging it to her bosom. 'Isn't it marvellous to think we've got Franz Liszt staying in the house?'

'Now, Louisa. Don't let's get hysterical.'

'I can't help it, I simply can't. And to *imagine* that he's going to live with us for always!'

'I beg your pardon?'

'Oh, Edward! I can hardly talk from excitement. And d'you know what I'm going to do next? Every musician in the whole world is going to want to meet him, that's a fact, and ask him about the people he knew – about Beethoven and Chopin and Schubert –'

'He can't talk,' her husband said.

'Well – all right. But they're going to want to meet him anyway, just to see him and touch him and to play their own music for him, modern music that he's never heard before.'

'He wasn't that great. Now, if it had been Bach or Beethoven ...'

'Don't interrupt, Edward, please. So what I'm going to do is to notify all of the important living composers everywhere. It's my duty. I'll tell them Liszt is here, and invite them to visit him. And you know what? They'll come flying in from every corner of the earth!'

'To see a grey cat?'

'Darling, it the same thing. It's *him*. No one cares what he *looks* like. Oh, Edward, it'll be the most exciting thing there ever was!'

They'll think you're mad.'

'You wait and see.' She was holding the cat in her arms and petting it tenderly but looking across at her husband, who now walked over to the French windows and stood there staring out into the garden. The evening was beginning, and the lawn was turning slowly from green to black, and in the distance he could see the smoke from his bonfire rising up in a white column.

'No' he said, without turning round, 'I'm not having it. Not in this house. It'll make us both look perfect fools.'

'Edward, what do you mean?'

'Just what I say. I absolutely refuse to have you stirring up a lot of publicity about a foolish thing like this. You happen to have found a trick cat. O.K. – that's fine. Keep it, if it pleases you. I don't mind. But I don't wish you to go any further than that. Do you understand me, Louisa?'

'Further than what?'

'I don't want to hear any more of this crazy talk. You're acting like a lunatic.'

Louisa put the cat slowly down on the sofa. Then slowly she raised herself to her full small height and took one pace forward. '*Damn* you, Edward!' she shouted, stamping her foot. 'For the first time in our lives something really exciting comes along and you're scared to death of having anything to do with it because someone may laugh at you! That's right, isn't it? You can't deny it, can you?'

'Louisa,' her husband said. 'That's quite enough of that. Pull yourself together now and stop this at once.' He walked over and took a cigarette from the box on the table, then lit it with the enormous patent lighter. His wife stood watching him, and now the tears were beginning to trickle out of the inside corners of her eyes, making two little shiny rivers where they ran through the powder on her cheeks.

'We've been having too many of these scenes just lately, Louisa,' he was saying. 'No no, don't interrupt. Listen to me. I make full allowance for the fact that this may be an awkward time of life for you, and that –'

'Oh, my God! You idiot! You pompous idiot! Can't you see that this is different, this is – this is something miraculous? Can't you see *that?*'

At that point, he came across the room and took her firmly by the shoulders. He had the freshly lit cigarette between his lips, and she could see faint contours on his skin where the heavy perspiration had dried in patches. 'Listen,' he said. 'I'm hungry. I've given up my golf and I've been working all day in the garden, and I'm tired and hungry and I want some supper. So do you. Off you go now to the kitchen and get us both something good to eat.'

Louisa stepped back and put both hands to her mouth. 'My heavens!' She cried. 'I forgot all about it. He must be absolutely famished. Except for some milk, I haven't given him a thing to eat since he arrived'.

'Who?'

'Why, *him*, of course. I must go at once and cook something really special. I wish I knew what his favourites dishes used to be. What do you think he would like best, Edward?'

'*Goddamn* it, Louisa!'

'Now, Edward, please. I'm going to handle this *my* way just for once. You stay here,' she said, bending down and touching the cat gently with her fingers. 'I won't be long.'

Louisa went into the kitchen and stood for a moment, wondering what special dish she might prepare. How about a soufflé? A nice cheese soufflé? Yes, that would be rather special. Of course, Edward didn't much care for them, but that couldn't be helped.

She was only a fair cook, and she couldn't be sure of always having a soufflé come out well, but she took extra trouble this time and waited a long while to make certain the oven had heated fully to the correct temperature. While the soufflé was baking and she was searching around for something to go with it, it occurred to her that Liszt had probably never in his life tasted either avocado pears or grapefruit, so she decided to give him both of them at once in a salad. It would be fun to watch his reaction. It really would.

When it was all ready, she put it on a tray and carried it into the living-room. At the exact moment she entered, she saw her husband coming in through the french windows from the garden.

'Here's his supper,' she said, putting it on the table and turning towards the sofa. 'Where is he?'

Her husband closed the garden door behind him and walked across the room to get himself a cigarette.

'Edward, where is he?'

'Who?'

'You know who.'

'Ah, yes. Yes, that's right. Well – I'll tell you.' He was bending forward to light the cigarette, and his hands were cupped around the enormous patent lighter. He glanced up and saw Louisa looking at him – at his shoes and the bottoms of his khaki slacks, which were damp from walking in long grass.

'I just went out to see how the bonfire was going,' he said.

Her eyes travelled slowly upward and rested on his hands.

'It's still burning fine,' he went on. 'I think it'll keep going all night.'

But the way she was staring made him uncomfortable.

'What is it?' he said, lowering the lighter. Then he looked down and noticed for the first time the long thin scratch that ran diagonally clear across the back of one hand, from the knuckle to the wrist.

'*Edward!*'

'Yes,' he said, 'I know. Those brambles are terrible. They tear you to pieces. Now, just a minute, Louisa. What's the matter?'

'*Edward!*'

'Oh, for God's sake, woman, sit down and keep calm. There's nothing to get worked up about, Louisa! Louisa, *sit down!*'

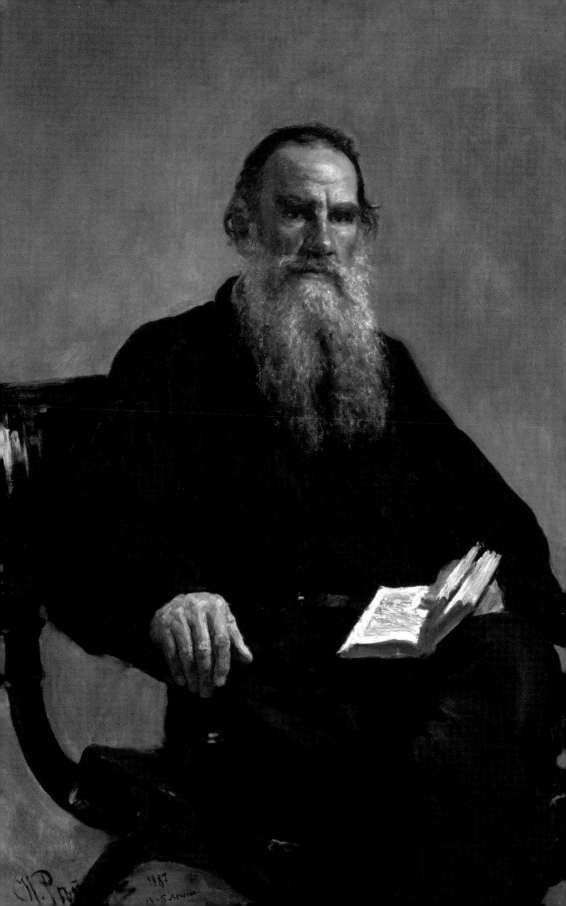

THE KREUTZER SONATA

Count Leo N. Tolstóy

"I THINK IT IS superfluous to say that I was very vainglorious: if we are not to be vainglorious in our habitual life, then there is no cause for living at all. Well, on that Sunday I entered with zest into the preparations for the dinner and soirée with the music. I myself bought things for the dinner and called the guests.

"At about six o'clock the guests arrived, and he appeared in evening dress with diamond studs, showing poor taste. He bore himself with ease, replied to everything hurriedly and with a slight smile of agreement and comprehension, – you know, with that especial expression which says that everything you may do or say is just what he expected. Everything which was improper in him I now took notice of with particular pleasure, because all this served to calm me and show me that he stood for my wife on a low level to which, as she said, she could not descend. I did not allow myself to be jealous. In the first place, my torment had been too great and I had to rest from it; in the second, I wished to believe the assertions of my wife, and I did believe them. And yet, although I was not jealous, I was unnatural toward him and toward her, and during the dinner and the first part of the evening entertainment, before the music began, I continued to watch their motions and glances.

"The dinner was like all dinners, – dull and stiff. The music began quite early. Oh, how I remember all the details of that evening! I remember how he brought the violin, opened the case, lifted the cover which had been embroidered for him by a lady, took out

Portrait of the author Leo N. Tolstóy (1828-1910) by Repin Ilya Yefimovich (1844-1930), Russia, 1887. State Tretyakov Gallery, Moscow. Oil on canvas.

the violin, and began to tune it. I remember how my wife sat down, feigning indifference, under which I saw her conceal her timidity, – timidity mainly as to her own ability, – how she sat down with a look of indifference at the piano, and there began the usual *la* on the piano, the pizzicato of the violin, and the placing of the music. I remember how, then, they looked at each other, casting a glance at the seated guests, how they said something one to the other, and how then it began. He took the first chords. His face grew serious, stern, and sympathetic, and, listening to his tones, he picked the strings with cautious fingers. The piano replied to him. And it began …"

Pózdnyshev stopped and several times in succession emitted his sounds. He wanted to speak, but he snuffled and again stopped.

"They were playing the Kreutzer Sonata by Beethoven," he continued. "Do you know the first presto? You do?" he exclaimed. "Ugh! Ugh! That sonata is a terrible thing, particularly that part of it. Music, in general, is a terrible thing. I cannot understand what it is. What is music? What does it do? And why does it do that which it does? They say that music acts upon the soul by elevating it, – nonsense, a lie! It acts, acts terribly, – I am speaking for myself, – but not at all by elevating. It neither elevates nor humbles the soul, – it irritates it. How shall I tell it to you? Music makes me forget myself and my real condition; it transfers me to another, not my own condition: it seems to me that under the influence of music I feel that which I really do not feel, that I understand that which I do not understand, that I can do that which I cannot do. I explain this by supposing that music acts like yawning, like laughter: I do not want to sleep, but I yawn seeing people yawn; I have no cause for laughing, but I laugh hearing others laugh.

"This music immediately, directly transfers me to the mental condition in which he was who wrote that music. I am merged in his soul, and am with him carried from one condition to another; but I do not know why this happens with me. He who wrote it, say the

'Kreutzer Sonata' by French artist René François Xavier Prinet (1861-1946), 1901, inspired by the novella by Leo Tolstóy, which had in turn been inspired by Beethoven's Violin Sonata No. 9, the 'Kreutzer Sonata'.

Kreutzer Sonata, – Beethoven, – he knew why he was in such a mood; this mood led him to do certain acts, and so this mood had some meaning for him, whereas for me it has none. Therefore music only irritates, – it does not end. Well, they play a military march, and the soldiers march under its strain, and the music comes to an end; they play dance music, and I finish dancing, and the music comes to an end; well, they sing a mass, I receive the Holy Sacrament, and the music comes to an end. But here there is only an irritation, but that which is to be done under this irritation is absent. It is for this reason that music is so terrible and often acts so dreadfully. In China music is a state matter. That is the way it ought to be. How can any one who wishes be allowed to hypnotize another, or many persons, and then do with them what he pleases? And especially how can they allow any kind of an immoral man to be the hypnotizer?

"Into whose hands has this terrible power fallen? Let us take for example the Kreutzer Sonata. How can one play the first presto in a drawing-room amidst ladies in décolleté garments? To play this presto, to applaud it, and then to eat ice-cream and talk about the last bit of gossip? These things should be played only under certain important, significant circumstances, and then when certain acts, corresponding to this music, are to be performed, and that is to be done which the music demands of you. But the provocation of energy and feeling which do not correspond to the time or place, and which find no expression, cannot help acting perniciously. Upon me, at least, it had a most terrible effect: it seemed to me as though entirely new feelings, new possibilities, of which I had never known before, were revealed to me. 'Yes, that is so, it is quite different from which I used to think and feel about it; it is like this,' a voice seemed to say within me. What this new thing was which I had discovered I was not able to explain to myself, but the consciousness of this new condition was a pleasurable one. All the people present – among them my wife and he – presented themselves in a new light to me.

"After the allegro they played the beautiful, but common, and not new andante with trite variations, and a very weak finale. After that they played, at the guests' request, an elegy by Ernst, and some other trifles. All that was very nice, but it did not produce on me one-hundredth part of the impression which the first had produced. All this took place on the background of the impression which had been evoked by the first piece.

"I felt light and happy on that evening. I had never before seen my wife as she was on that evening. Those sparkling eyes, that severity and expressiveness while she was playing, and that complete dis-solution, if I may so call it, and that feeble, pitiable, and blissful smile after they were through! I saw it all, but ascribed no other meaning to it than that she was experiencing the same as I, and that to her, as to me, there were revealed, or, as it were, brought back, new, unfelt sensations. The evening came to a successful end and all departed.

"Knowing that I was to leave in two days to attend to the meeting, Trukhachévski at leaving said that he hoped at his next visit to repeat the pleasure of the present evening. From this I could conclude that he did not consider it possible to be in my house during my absence, and this pleased me.

"It turned out that since I should not be back before his departure, we should not meet again.

"I for the first time pressed his hand with real joy and thanked him for the pleasure he had given me. He, too, bade farewell to my wife. Their farewell seemed to me most natural and proper. Everything was beautiful. My wife and I were both very much satisfied with the evening."

SWANN IN LOVE

Marcel Proust

THE YEAR BEFORE, at an evening party, he had heard a piece of music played on the piano and violin. At first he had appreciated only the material quality of the sounds which those instruments secreted. And it had been a source of keen pleasure when, below the narrow ribbon of the violin-part, delicate, unyielding, substantial and governing the whole, he had suddenly perceived, where it was trying to surge upwards in a flowing tide of sound, the mass of the piano-part, multiform, coherent, level, and breaking everywhere in melody like the deep blue tumult of the sea, silvered and charmed into a minor key by the moonlight. But at a given moment, without being able to distinguish any clear outline, or to give a name to what was pleasing him, suddenly enraptured, he had tried to collect, to treasure in his memory the phrase or harmony – he knew not which – that had just been played, and had opened and expanded his soul, just as the fragrance of certain roses, wafted upon the moist air of evening, has the power of dilating our nostrils. Perhaps it was owing to his own ignorance of music that he had been able to receive so confused an impression, one of those that are, notwithstanding, our only purely musical impressions, limited in their extent, entirely original, and irreducible into any other kind. An impression of this order, vanishing in an instant, is, so to speak, an impression *sine material*. Presumably the notes which we hear at such moments tend to spread out before our eyes over surfaces greater or smaller according to their pitch and volume; to trace arabesque designs, to

Portrait of the French novelist Marcel Proust (1871-1922) by Jacques-Emile Blanche (1861-1942). Oil on canvas. Paris, Musee d'Orsay.

give us the sensation of breath or tenuity, stability or caprice. But the notes themselves have vanished before these sensations have developed sufficiently to escape submersion under those which the following, or even simultaneous notes have already begun to awaken in us. And this indefinite perception would continue to smother in its molten liquidity the *motifs* which now and then emerge, barely discernible, to plunge again and disappear and drown; recognised only by the particular kind of pleasure which they instil, impossible to describe, to recollect, to name; ineffable; – if our memory, like a labourer who toils at the laying down of firm foundations beneath the tumult of the waves, did not, by fashioning for us facsimiles of those fugitive phrases, enable us to compare and to contrast them with those that follow. And so, hardly had the delicious sensation, which Swann had experienced, died away, before his memory had furnished him with an immediate transcript, summary, it is true, and provisional, but one on which he had kept his eyes fixed while the playing continued, so effectively that, when the same impression suddenly returned, it was no longer uncapturable. He was able to picture to himself its extent, its symmetrical arrangement, its notation, the strength of its expression; he had before him that definite object which was no longer pure music, but rather design architecture, thought, and which allowed the actual music to be recalled. This time he had distinguished, quite clearly, a phrase which emerged for a few moments from the waves of sound. It had at once held out to him an invitation to partake of intimate pleasures, of whose existence, before hearing it, he had never dreamed, into which he felt that nothing but this phrase could initiate him; and he had been filled with love for it, as with a new and strange desire.

With a slow and rhythmical movement it led him here, there, everywhere, towards a state of happiness noble, unintelligible, yet clearly indicated. And then, suddenly having reached a certain point from which he was prepared to follow it, after pausing for a moment, abruptly it changed its direction, and in a fresh movement, more rapid, multiform, melancholy, incessant, sweet, it bore him off with it towards a vista of joys unknown. Then it vanished. He hoped, with a passionate longing, that he might find it again, a third time. And reappear it did, though without speaking to him more clearly, bringing him, indeed, a pleasure less profound. But when he was once more at home he needed it, he was like a man into whose life a woman, whom he has seen for a moment passing by, has brought a new form of beauty, which strengthens and enlarges his own power of perception, without his knowing even whether he is ever to see her again whom he loves already, although he knows nothing of her, not even her name.

Indeed, this passion for a phrase of music seemed, in the first few months, to be bringing into Swann's life the possibility of a sort of rejuvenation. He had so long since ceased to direct his course towards any ideal goal, and had confined himself to the pursuit of ephemeral satisfaction, that he had come to believe, though without ever formally stating his belief even to himself, that he would remain all his life in that condition, which death alone could alter. More than this, since his mind no longer entertained any lofty ideals, he had ceased to believe in (although he could not have expressly denied) their reality. He had grown also into the habit of taking refuge in trivial considerations, which allowed him to set on one side matters of fundamental importance. Just as he had never stopped to ask himself whether he would have not done better by not going into society, knowing very well that if he had accepted an invitation he must put in an appearance, and that afterwards, if he did not actually call, he must at least leave cards upon his hostess; so in his conversation he took care never to express with any warmth a personal opinion about a thing, but instead would supply facts and details which had a value of a sort in themselves, and excused him from shewing how much he really knew. He would be extremely precise about the recipe for a dish, the dates of a painter's birth and death, and the titles of his works. Sometimes, in spite of himself, he would let himself go so far as to utter a criticism of a work of art, or of some one's interpretation of life, but then he would cloak his words in a tone of irony, as though he did not altogether associate himself with what he was saying. But now, like a confirmed invalid whom, all of a sudden, a change of air and surroundings, or a new course of treatment, or, as sometimes happens, an organic change in himself, spontaneous and unaccountable, seems to have so far recovered from his malady that he begins to envisage the possibility, hitherto beyond all hope, of starting to lead – and better late than never – a wholly different life, Swann found in himself, in the memory of the phrase that he had heard, in certain other sonatas which he had made people play over to him, to see whether he might not, perhaps, discover his phrase among them, the presence of one of those invisible realities in which he had ceased to believe, but to which, as though the music had had upon the moral barrenness from which he was suffering a sort of recreative influence, he was conscious once again of a desire, almost, indeed, of the power to consecrate his life. But, never having managed to find out whose work it was that he had heard played that evening, he had been unable to procure a copy, and finally had forgotten the quest. He had indeed, in the course of the next few days, encountered several of the people who had been at the party with him, and had questioned them; but most of them had either arrived after or left before the piece was played; some had indeed been in the house, but had gone into another room to talk, and those who had stayed to listen had no clearer impression than the rest. As for his hosts, they knew that it was a recently published work which the musicians whom they had engaged for the evening had asked to be allowed to play; but, as these last were now on tour somewhere, Swann could learn nothing further. He had, of course, a number of musical friends, but, vividly as he could recall the exquisite and inexpressible pleasure which the little phrase had given him, and could see, still, before his eyes the forms that it had traced in outline, he was quite incapable of humming over to them the air. And so, at last, he ceased to think of it.

ROTHSCHILD'S FIDDLE

Anton Chekhov

IT WAS A TINY TOWN, worse than a village, inhabited chiefly by old people who so seldom died that it was really vexatious. Very few coffins were needed for the hospital and the jail; in a word, business was bad. If Jacob Ivanoff had been a maker of coffins in the county town, he would probably have owned a house of his own by now, and would have been called Mr Ivanoff, but here in this little place he was simply called Jacob, and for some reason his nickname was Bronze. He lived as poorly as any common peasant in a little old hut of one room, in which he and Martha, and the stove, and a double bed, and the coffins, and his joiner's bench, and all the necessities of housekeeping were stowed away.

The coffins made by Jacob were serviceable and strong. For the peasants and townsfolk he made them to fit himself and never went wrong, for, although he was seventy years old, there was no man, not even in the prison, any taller or stouter than he was. For the gentry and for women he made them to measure, using an iron yardstick for the purpose. He was always very reluctant to take orders for children's coffins, and made them contemptuously without taking any measurements at all, always saying when he was paid for them:

"The fact is, I don't like to be bothered with trifles."

Besides what he received for his work as a joiner, he added a little to his income by playing the violin. There was a Jewish orchestra in the town that played for weddings, led by the tinsmith Moses Shakess, who took more than half of its earnings for himself. As

Portrait of the Russian author Anton Chekhov (1860-1904) by Braz Osip Emmanuilovich (1872-1936), 1898. State Tretyakov Gallery, Moscow. Oil on canvas.

Jacob played the fiddle extremely well, especially Russian songs, Shakess used sometimes to invite him to play in his orchestra for the sum of fifty kopecks a day, not including the presents he might receive from the guests. Whenever Bronze took his seat in the orchestra, the first thing that happened to him was that his face grew red, and the perspiration streamed from it, for the air was always hot, and reeking of garlic to the point of suffocation. Then his fiddle would begin to moan, and a double bass would croak hoarsely into his right ear, and a flute would weep into his left. The flute was played by a gaunt, red-bearded Jew with a network of red and blue veins on his face, who bore the name of a famous rich man, Rothschild. This confounded Jew always contrived to play even the merriest of tunes sadly. For no obvious reasons Jacob little by little began to conceive a feeling of hatred and contempt for all Jews, and especially for Rothschild. He quarrelled with him and abused him in ugly language, and once even tried to beat him, but Rothschild took offence at this, and cried with a fierce look:

"If I had not always respected you for your music, I should have thrown you out of the window long ago!"

Then he burst into tears. So after that Bronze was not invited to play in the orchestra, and was only called upon in case of dire necessity, when one of the Jews was missing.

Jacob was never in a good humor, because he always had to endure the most terrible losses. For instance, it was a sin to work on a Sunday or a holiday, and Monday was always a bad day, so in that way there were about two hundred days a year in which he was compelled to sit with his hands folded in his lap. That was a great loss to him. If any one in town had a wedding without music, or if Shakess did not ask him to play, there was another loss. The police inspector had lain ill with consumption for two years while Jacob impatiently waited for him to die, and then had gone to take a cure in the city and had died there, which of course meant another loss of at least ten roubles, as the coffin would have been an expensive one lined with brocade.

The thought of his losses worried Jacob at night more than at any other time, so he used to lay his fiddle at his side on the bed, and when those worries came trooping into his brain he would touch the strings, and the fiddle would give out a sound in the darkness, and Jacob's heart would feel lighter.

Last year on the sixth of May, Martha suddenly fell ill. The woman breathed with difficulty, staggered in her walk, and felt terribly thirsty. Nevertheless, she got up that morning, lit the stove, and even went for the water. When evening came she went to bed. Jacob played his fiddle all day. When it grew quite dark, because he had nothing better to do, he took the book in which he kept an account of his losses, and began adding up the total for the year. They amounted to more than a thousand roubles. He was so shaken by this discovery that he threw the counting board on the floor and trampled it under foot. Then he picked it up again and rattled it once more for a long time, heaving as he did so sighs both deep and long. His face grew purple, and perspiration dripped from his brow. He was thinking that if those thousand roubles he had lost had been in the bank then, he would have had at least forty roubles interest by the end of the year. So those forty roubles were still another loss! In a word, wherever he turned he found losses and nothing but losses.

"Jacob!" cried Martha unexpectedly, "I am going to die!"

He looked round at his wife. Her face was flushed with fever and looked unusually joyful and bright. Bronze was troubled, for he had been accustomed to seeing her pale and timid and unhappy. It seemed to him that she was actually dead, and glad to have left this hut, and the coffins, and Jacob at last. She was staring at the ceiling, with her lips moving as if she saw her deliverer Death approaching and were whispering with him.

The dawn was just breaking and the eastern sky was glowing with a faint radiance. As he stared at the old woman it somehow seemed to Jacob that he had never once spoken a tender word to her or pitied her; that he had never thought of buying her a kerchief or of bringing her back some sweetmeats from a wedding. On the contrary, he had shouted at her and abused her for his losses, and had shaken his fist at her. It was true he had never beaten her, but he had frightened her no less, and she had been paralyzed with fear every time he had scolded her. Yes, and he had not allowed her to drink tea because his losses were heavy enough as it was, so she had to be content with hot water. Now he understood why her face looked so strangely happy, and horror overwhelmed him.

As soon as it was light he borrowed a horse from a neighbour and took Martha to the hospital. As there were not many patients, he had not to wait very long – only about three hours. To his great satisfaction it was not the doctor who was receiving the sick that day, but his assistant, Maksim Nicolaitch, an old man of whom it was said that, although he quarrelled and drank, he knew more than the doctor did.

"Good morning, Your Honor," said Jacob leading his old woman into the office. "Excuse us for intruding upon you with our trifling affairs. As you see, this subject has fallen ill. My life's friend, if you will allow me to use the expression ..."

Knitting his grey eyebrows and stroking his whiskers, the doctor's assistant fixed his eyes on the old woman. She was sitting all in a heap on a low stool, and with her thin, long-nosed face and her open mouth, she looked like a thirsty bird.

"Well, well – yes ..." said the doctor slowly, heaving a sigh. "This is a case of influenza and possibly fever; there is typhoid in town. What's to be done? The old woman has lived her span of years, thank God. How old is she?"

"She lacks one year of being seventy, Your Honor."

"Well, well, she has lived long. There must come an end to everything."

"You are certainly right, Your Honor," said Jacob, smiling out of politeness. "And we thank you sincerely for your kindness, but allow me to suggest to you that even an insect dislikes to die!"

"Never mind if it does!" answered the doctor, as if the life or death of the old woman lay in his hands. "I'll tell you what you must do, my good man. Put a cold bandage around her head, and give her two of these powders a day. Now then, good-bye! *Bon jour!*"

Jacob saw by the expression on the doctor's face that it was too late now for powders. He realized clearly that Martha must die very soon, if not today, then tomorrow. He touched the doctor's elbow gently, blinked and whispered:

"She ought to be cupped, doctor!"

"I haven't time, I haven't time, my good man. Take your old woman, and go in God's name. Good-bye."

"Please, please, cup her, doctor!" begged Jacob. "You know yourself that if she had a pain in her stomach, powders and drops would do her good, but she has a cold! The first thing to do when one catches cold is to let some blood, doctor!"

But the doctor had already sent for the next patient, and a woman leading a little boy came into the room.

"Go along, go along!" he cried to Jacob, frowning. "It's no use making a fuss!"

"Then at least put some leeches on her. Let me pray to God for you for the rest of my life!"

The doctor's temper flared up and he shouted:

"Don't say another word to me, blockhead!"

Jacob lost his temper, too, and flushed hotly, but he said nothing and, silently taking Martha's arm, led her out of the office. Only when they were once more seated in their wagon did he look fiercely and mockingly at the hospital and say:

"They're a pretty lot in there, they are! That doctor would have cupped a rich man, but he even begrudged a poor one a leech. The pig!"

When they returned to the hut, Martha stood for nearly ten minutes supporting herself by the stove. She felt that if she lay down Jacob would begin to talk to her about his losses, and would scold her for lying down and not wanting to work. Jacob contemplated her sadly, thinking that tomorrow was St. John the Baptist's day, and day after tomorrow was St. Nicholas the Wonder-Worker's day, and that the following day would be Sunday, and the day after that would be Monday, a bad day for work. So he would not be able to work for four days, and as Martha would probably die on one of these days, the coffin would have to be made at once. He took his iron yardstick in hand, went up to the old woman, and measured her. Then she lay down, and he crossed himself and went to work on the coffin.

When the task was completed Bronze put on his spectacles and wrote in his book:

"For 1 coffin for Martha Ivanoff – 2 roubles, 40 copecks."

He sighed. All day the old woman lay silent with closed eyes, but toward evening, when the daylight began to fade, she suddenly called the old man to her side.

"Do you remember, Jacob?" she asked. "Do you remember how fifty years ago God gave us a little baby with curly golden hair? Do you remember how you and I used to sit on the bank of the river and sing songs under the willow tree?" Then with a bitter smile she added: "The baby died."

Jacob racked his brains, but for the life of him he could not recall the child or the willow tree.

"You are dreaming," he said.

The priest came and administered the Sacrament and Extreme Unction. Then Martha began muttering unintelligibly, and toward morning she died.

The neighbouring old women washed her and dressed her, and laid her in the coffin. To avoid paying the deacon, Jacob read the psalms over her himself, and her grave cost him nothing as the watchman of the cemetery was his cousin. Four peasants carried the coffin to the grave, not for money but for love. The old women, the beggars, and two village idiots followed the body, and the people whom they passed on the way crossed themselves devoutly. Jacob was very glad that everything had passed off so nicely and decently and cheaply, without giving offence to any one. As he said farewell to Martha for the last time he touched the coffin with his hand and thought:

"That's a fine job!"

But walking homeward from the cemetery he was seized with great distress. He felt ill, his breath was burning hot, his legs grew weak, and he longed for a drink. Beside this, a thousand thoughts came crowding into his head. He remembered again that he had never once pitied Martha or said a tender word to her. The fifty years of their life together lay stretched far, far behind him, and somehow, during all that time, he had never once thought about her at all or noticed her more than if she had been a dog or a cat. And yet she had lit the stove every day, and had cooked and baked and fetched water and chopped wood, and when he had come home drunk from a wedding she had hung his fiddle reverently on a nail each time, and had silently put him to bed with a timid, anxious look on her face.

But here came Rothschild toward him, bowing and scraping and smiling.

"I have been looking for you, uncle!" he said. "Moses Shakess presents his compliments and wants you to go to him at once."

Jacob did not feel in a mood to do anything. He wanted to cry.

"Leave me alone!" he exclaimed, and walked on.

"Oh, how can you say that?" cried Rothschild, running beside him in alarm. "Moses will be very angry. He wants you to come at once!"

Jacob was disgusted by the panting of the Jew, by his blinking eyes, and by the quantities of reddish freckles on his face. He looked with aversion at his long green coat and at the whole of his frail, delicate figure.

"What do you mean by pestering me, garlic?" he shouted. "Get away!"

The Jew grew angry and shouted back:

"Don't yell at me like that or I'll send you flying over that fence!"

"Get out of my sight!" bellowed Jacob, shaking his fist at him. "There's no living in the same town with swine like you!"

Rothschild was petrified with terror. He sank to the ground and waved his hands over his head as if to protect himself from falling blows; then he jumped up and ran away as fast as his legs could carry him. As he ran he leaped and waved his arms, and his long, gaunt back could be seen quivering. The little boys were delighted at what had happened, and ran after him screaming: "Sheeny! Sheeny!" The dogs also joined barking in the chase. Somebody laughed and then whistled, at which the dogs barked louder and more vigorously than ever.

Then one of them must have bitten Rothschild, for a piteous, despairing scream rent the air.

Jacob walked across the common to the edge of the town without knowing where he was going, and the little boys shouted after him. "There goes old man Bronze! There goes old man Bronze!" He found himself by the river where the snipe were darting about with shrill cries, and the ducks were quacking and swimming to and fro. The sun was shining fiercely and the water was sparkling so brightly that it was painful to look at. Jacob struck into a path that led along the riverbank. He came to a stout, red-cheeked woman just leaving a bath-house. "Aha, you otter, you!" he thought. Not far from the bath-house some little boys were fishing for crabs with pieces of meat. When they saw Jacob they shouted mischievously:

"Old man Bronze! Old man Bronze!" But there before him stood an ancient, spreading willow tree with a massive trunk, and a crow's nest among its branches. Suddenly there flashed across Jacob's memory with all the vividness of life a little child with golden curls, and the willow of which Martha had spoken. Yes, this was the same tree, so green and peaceful and sad. How old it had grown, poor thing.

He sat down at its foot and thought of the past. On the opposite shore, where that meadow now was, there had stood in those days a wood of tall birch-trees, and that bare hill on the horizon yonder had been covered with the blue bloom of an ancient pine forest. And sailboats had plied the river then, but now all lay smooth and still, and only one little birch-tree was left on the opposite bank, a graceful young thing, like a girl, while on the river there swam only ducks and geese. It was hard to believe that boats had once sailed there. It seemed to him that there were fewer geese now than there had been. Jacob shut his eyes, and one by one white geese came flying toward him, an endless flock.

He was puzzled to know why he had never once been down to the river during the last forty or fifty years of his life, or, if he had been there, why he had never paid any attention to it. The stream was fine and large; he might have fished in it and sold the fish to the merchants and the government officials and the restaurant-keeper at the station, and put the money in the bank. He might have rowed in a boat from farm to farm and played on his fiddle. People of every rank would have paid him money to hear him. He might have tried to run a boat on the river, that would have been better than making coffins. Finally, he might have raised geese, and killed them, and sent them to Moscow in the winter. Why, the down alone would have brought him ten roubles a year! But he had missed all those chances and had done nothing. What losses were here! Ah, what terrible losses! And, oh, if he had only done all these things at the same time!

If he had only fished, and played the fiddle, and sailed a boat, and raised geese, what capital he would have had by now! But he had not even dreamed of doing all this; his life had gone by without profit or pleasure. It had been lost for a song. Nothing was left ahead; behind lay only losses, and such terrible losses that he shuddered to think of them. But why shouldn't men live so as to avoid all this waste and these losses? Why, oh why, should those birch and pine forests have been felled? Why should those meadows be lying so deserted? Why did people always do exactly what they ought not to do? Why had Jacob scolded and growled and clenched his fists and hurt his wife's feelings all his life? Why, oh why, had he frightened and insulted that Jew just now? Why did people in general always interfere with one another? What losses resulted from this! What terrible losses! If it were not for envy and anger they would get great profit from one another.

All that evening and night Jacob dreamed of the child, of the willow tree, of the fish and the geese, of Martha with her profile like a thirsty bird, and of Rothschild's pale, piteous mien. Queer faces seemed to be moving toward him from all sides, muttering to him about his losses. He tossed from side to side and got up five times during the night to play his fiddle.

He rose with difficulty next morning, and walked to the hospital. The same doctor's assistant ordered him to put cold bandages on his head, and gave him little powders to take; by his expression and the tone of his voice Jacob knew that the state of affairs was bad, and that no powders could save him now. As he walked home he reflected that one good thing would result from his death; he would no longer have to eat and drink and pay taxes, neither would he offend people any more, and, as a man lies in his grave for hundreds of thousands of years, the sum of his profits would be immense. So, life to a man was a loss – death, a gain. Of course this reasoning was correct, but it was also distressingly sad. Why should the world be so strangely arranged that a man's life which was only given to him once must pass without profit?

He was not sorry then that he was going to die, but when he reached home, and saw his fiddle, his heart ached, and he regretted it deeply. He would not be able to take his fiddle with him into the grave, and now it would be left an orphan, and its fate would be that of the birch grove and pine forest. Everything in the world had been lost, and would always be lost for ever. Jacob went out and sat on the threshold of his hut, clasping his fiddle to his breast. And as he thought of his life so full of waste and losses he began playing without knowing how piteous and touching his music was, and the tears streamed down his cheeks. And the more he thought the more sorrowfully sang his violin.

The latch clicked and Rothschild came in through the garden gate, and walked boldly halfway across the garden. Then he suddenly stopped, crouched down, and, probably from fear, began making signs with his hands as if he were trying to show on his fingers what time it was.

"Come on, don't be afraid!" said Jacob gently, beckoning him to advance. "Come on!"

With many mistrustful and fearful glances Rothschild went slowly up to Jacob, and stopped about two yards away.

"Please don't beat me!" he said with a ducking bow. "Moses Shakess has sent me to you again. 'Don't be afraid,' he said, 'go to Jacob,' says he, 'and say that we can't possibly manage without him.' There is to be a wedding next Thursday. Ye-es sir. Mr Shapovaloff is marrying his daughter to a very fine man. It will be an expensive wedding, ai, ai!" added the Jew with a wink.

"I can't go" said Jacob breathing hard. "I'm ill, brother."

And he began to play again, and the tears gushed out of his eyes over his fiddle. Rothschild listened intently with his head turned away and his arms folded on his breast. The startled, irresolute look on his face gradually gave way to one of suffering and grief. He cast up his eyes as if in an ecstasy of agony and murmured: "Ou-ouch!" And the tears began to trickle slowly down his cheeks, and to drip over his green coat.

All day Jacob lay and suffered. When the priest came in the evening to administer the Sacrament he asked him if he could not think of any particular sin.

Struggling with his fading memories, Jacob recalled once more Martha's sad face, and the despairing cry of the Jew when the dog had bitten him. He murmured almost inaudibly:

"Give my fiddle to Rothschild."

"It shall be done," answered the priest.

So it happened that everyone in the little town began asking:

"Where did Rothschild get that good fiddle? Did he buy it or steal it or get it out of a pawnshop?"

Rothschild has long since abandoned his flute, and now only plays on the violin. The same mournful notes flow from under his bow that used to come from his flute, and when he tries to repeat what Jacob played as he sat on the threshold of his hut, the result is an air so plaintive and sad that everyone who hears him weeps, and he himself at last raises his eyes and murmurs: "Oo-ouch!" And this new song has so delighted the town that the merchants and government officials vie with each other in getting Rothschild to come to their houses, and sometimes make him play it ten times in succession.

AN ARGUMENT FOR
RICHARD STRAUSS

Glenn Gould

A FRIEND OF MINE once remarked that there was probably a
moment in every budding musician's teen-age years when *Ein
Heldenleben* might suddenly appear the work most likely to incor-
porate all of the doubts, and stresses, and the hoped-for triumphs of
youth. He was only half-serious I suppose, but I think he was also
half-right; and, although he didn't intend it disparagingly, his remark
did suggest the assumption that if one could grow naturally into a
sympathy with the flamboyant extroversion of the young Richard
Strauss, so one could be expected, with maturity, to grow just as
naturally out of it. My own *Heldenleben* period began, courtesy of
Willem Mengelberg, when I was seventeen, but – although I have
now patiently waited twelve years – I have never grown out of it. And
though it may well be a damning commentary on the waywardness
of my own maturing, I rather doubt if I ever shall!

So it is not easy for me to write objectively about Richard Strauss,
although I intend to try to do so, however, because I write from a
position of high prejudice; I believe, quite simply, that Strauss was
the greatest musical figure who has lived in this century. This is not
a very welcome view today, because, although Strauss does not
really need anyone to extol his merits to the world, his reputation
has perhaps suffered more unjustly with the passing years than that
of any other musician of our time. At first glance, this may appear
a rather surprising statement, since Strauss has never been more

Portrait of German composer Richard Georg Strauss (Munich, 1864-
Garmisch-Partenkirchen, 1949) by Max Liebermann (1847-1935).

frequently or devotedly favoured in performance than at present, but I am referring now not to those Teutonic lions of the podium, who nightly soar from our midst to be with Zarathustra on his mountain-top, nor do I speak of those artful tigresses of the operatic stage for whom no greater challenge nor surer success exists than that which Chrysothemis or the Marschallin assures. I refer, rather, to those cunning currents of fancy which, as they sweep to command the tide of musical taste, make haste to consign old Strauss to the graveyard for romantics, pronouncing him a great nineteenth-century character who had the audacity to live fifty years into the twentieth.

The longevity of Strauss's creative life is pretty staggering, of course – at least sixty-nine years if one reckons his adolescent works as the astonishing creations they really are, or in other words, a span equal to the total lifetimes of two Mozarts (if you have a head for that sort of thing). Now, obviously, the length of Strauss's creative life is not important of itself – many composers plan to live to one hundred and six, while I myself aim to withdraw into a graceful autumnal senility at thirty. Yet the longevity of a creative life is a justifiable yardstick within the extent that it measures, and can be measured by, the development of the composer as a human being.

It is the view shaped by the tastemakers of the musical profession that Strauss's evolution as a musician was not consistent with the length of his years. They seem to feel that his development was arrested somewhere within the first decade of this century. They do not always deny him the achievement of his early works: some of them can even whistle a few tunes from the tone poems, and many will admit the dramatic values of his first great operatic successes – the charm and gallantry of *Rosenkavalier*, the strangling impact of *Electra*. But most of them seem to think that having made himself for twenty-five years or so a bulwark of the avant-garde, Strauss in his mid-forties lapsed into a drought of inspiration which was terminated only by his death.

Is it a curious accident, I wonder, that the point in Strauss's career at which, with the precision of hindsight, he is presumed to have gone astray is more or less concurrent with the beginning of the most significant musical revolution (or if you prefer, reformation) of modern times, the development of the musical language without tonality? Or is it just coincidence that even well-informed opinion sees Strauss as having reached the climax of his career just prior to those years in which other composers first broke through the sonic barriers of tonal harmony, and that when he appeared to reject the new aesthetic, the tastemakers and the pacesetters would see him only as a man wistfully attempting to recapitulate the achievements of his youth?

The generation, or rather the generations, that have grown up since the early years of this century have considered the most serious of Strauss's errors to be his failure to share actively in the technical advances of his time. They hold that having once evolved a uniquely identifiable means of expression, and having expressed himself within it at first with all the joys of high adventure, he had thereafter, from the technical point of view, appeared to remain stationary – simply saying again and again that which in the energetic days of his youth he had said with so much greater strength and clarity. For these critics it is inconceivable that a man of such gifts would not wish to participate in the expansion of the musical language, that a man who had the good fortune to be writing masterpieces in the days of Brahms and Bruckner and the luck to live beyond Webern into the age of Boulez and Stockhausen should not want to search out his own place in the great adventure of musical evolution. What must one do to convince such folk that art is not technology, that the difference between a Richard Strauss and a Karlheinz Stockhausen is not comparable to the differences between a humble office adding machine and an IBM computer?

Richard Strauss, then, seems to me to be more than the greatest man of music of our time. He is in my opinion a central figure in today's most crucial dilemma of aesthetic morality – the hopeless confusion that arises when we attempt to contain the inscrutable pressures of self-guiding artistic destiny within the neat, historical summation of collective chronology. He is much more than a convenient rallying point for conservative opinion. In him we have one of those rare, intense figures in whom the whole process of historical evolution is defied.

Throughout those seven working decades the most striking common feature of Strauss's work is the extraordinary consistency of his vocabulary. One can compare, to take virtually the extreme instance, his Symphony, Op. 12, written when he was eighteen, and the *Metamorphosen* for string orchestra, written at the age of eighty-one, and one will have to admit that neither contains any harmonic progression which would have been necessarily unavailable to the other. Basically, both use a harmonic language available to Brahms, or to Hugo Wolf, or, minus his sequences, to Bruckner; both use a contrapuntal style which, although more in evidence in the later work, is still primarily founded upon the belief that, however many contrarieties it may provoke, its fundamental duty is to substantiate the harmonic motion and not to contradict it. And yet for all these similarities the *Metamorphosen* conveys the impression of an altogether different harmonic and contrapuntal scope than the Symphony, and both suggest a unique identity which could not possibly be confused with any earlier master. While there are pages in the teen-age works of Strauss (the First Horn Concerto, for instance) which, at a diagrammatic harmonic level, could easily have been written by Mendelssohn, or even, surprisingly, by Weber, one needs only a few seconds to realize that here, for all the influence of the early romantic masters, is a wholly original technique.

Although he reached adolescence at a time when Wagner had anticipated the dissolution of the tonal language and had stretched the cognizance of harmonic psychology to a point that some regarded as the very limit of human endurance, Strauss perhaps was more concerned than any other composer of his generation with utilizing the fullest riches of late romantic tonality *within* the firmest possible formal disciplines. With Strauss it was not simply a question of compensating for the overrich harmonic ambiguities of his era (as was the case with the intense motivic concentration of the young Arnold Schoenberg): rather, his interest was primarily the preservation of the *total* function of tonality – not simply in a work's fundamental outline but even in its most specific minutiae of design. Consequently, when one compares any of Strauss's early orchestral scores with, say, a tone poem by Liszt, one is immediately struck with the fact that while Strauss's works demonstrate infinitely greater daring in terms of sheer extravagance of harmonic imagination, they are nevertheless painstakingly explicit at every level of their architectural concept and thus present an impression of a harmonic language at once more varied and more lucid. With this immense harmonic resource laboring within what is frequently an almost rococo sense of line and ornamentation, Strauss is able to produce by the simplest and almost deceptively familiar means an overpowering emotional effect. Who else is able to make the bland orthodoxies of a cadential six-four seem a wholly delectable extravagance?

Rarely among the German romantics is there writing that matches the glorious harmonic infallibility of the young Strauss. Among his predecessors only Mendelssohn and Brahms in their best pages were as conscious of the need to strengthen the vagrant structures of romantic tonality through the emphatic control and direction of the harmonic bass. One would almost suspect that Strauss conceived of the cellos and basses with his feet (as an organist might do), for at every moment – regardless of the breadth of the score, regardless of its metric complexities, regardless of the kaleidoscopic cross-reference of chromatic tonality – the bass line remains as firm, as secure, a counterpoise as in the works of Bach or of Palestrina.

It must not be supposed that striving in this way for the ultimate accentuation of linear clarity led Strauss into the contrapuntist's concern for a linear texture which accords to each voice its own independent existence. Strauss was by no means a composer who practised counterpoint per se. In his music the absolute contrapuntal forms – the fugue, the canon, etc. – appear primarily in the operas (and even there infrequently) and are almost without exception the occasion for a self-conscious underlining of the libretto. Such occasions are, from a purely academic point of view, quite beyond criticism, but one always has the feeling that Strauss is saying, "Look, see, I can do it, too!" and that he regards such diversions simply as a means to enliven an otherwise static situation on the stage; and yet, although in the vast body of Strauss's work there are few examples of the sort of contrapuntal devices which most other twentieth-century composers, in their search for motivic interrelation, have used constantly, it cannot be overemphasized that Strauss, on his own terms, was among the most contrapuntal minded of composers.

The fundamental strength of Strauss's counterpoint does not lie in his ability to provide an autonomous existence for each voice within the symmetric structure – his whole symphonic orientation is too thoroughly nineteenth-century to make this either possible or, to his mind, I suppose, desirable. Rather, it lies in his ability to create a sense of poetic relation between the soaring, dexterous soprano melodies, the firm, reflective, always cadential-minded basses, and most important of all, the superbly filigreed texture of his inner voices. There are many more contradictory stresses in the linear designs of Strauss than in Wagner, for instance, whose accumulation of density tend to have perhaps more singlemindedness, more uniformity of stress and relaxation, than do those of Strauss; but by the very mixture of this finely chiselled contrapuntal style and this

vastly complex harmonic language, Strauss's climaxes, his moments of tension and of repose, are – if less overwhelming than those of Wagner – infinitely more indicative of the complex realities of art.

When he came under Wagner's influence, Strauss inherited the problem of translating the dramatic possibilities of the former's harmonic freedom into the realm of symphonic music; for Strauss not only began his career as a symphonist (indeed, at first, a symphonist of a particularly straitlaced order) but was, with all his sovereign mastery of the stage, a man who always thought primarily in symphonic terms. The problem of developing a musical architecture that would relate somehow to the extravagance of a richly chromatic tonality and would make use of all the ambiguities contained there was, of course, the primary problem for all the composers of Strauss's generation. It was simply unsatisfactory to shape symphonic creations within the mold of the classical sonata structures with all the implied tonal plateaus which tradition begged if one wanted to use material chosen less for its thematic profile than for its genetical probabilities. (The problem was certainly less serious for Strauss that it was for Schoenberg, who seems always to have had a more relentless determination to exhaust all motivic permutations.)

The young Strauss sought a solution in the symphonic poem, in which the logic of the musical contours would stand in supposed relation to a predetermined plot exposition that could suggest the texture, the duration, and the tonal plateaus of each episode. It was at best a halfway logic, for most listeners are almost certainly little aware of the legal embarrassments of Till Eulenspiegel or the philosophic posings of Zarathustra and likely care even less. Probably they recognize, or try to, those correspondences with the purely symphonic structures which Strauss sought to supplant. What is more to the point about the tone-poem logic is that in Strauss's mind it provided a sense of architectural cohesion which might not need to be externally observed. Thus an entirely musical logic, which was always present, was simply reinforced at conception by a pseudo-dramatic one that, having fulfilled its role, could easily be abandoned at birth. The entangling of musical events with dramatic ones is a risky business; and although Strauss took great pride in his ability to describe extramusical circumstances musically (a talent which was later to make him the greatest operatic composer of his time), the essence of the tone poem structure did not depend on the circumstance that a series of dramatic occurrences appear in a recognizable paraphrase. Rather, it lay in the fact that the harmony of dramatic events could be used as a focus for musical form. (Fascinating that Thomas Mann was always talking about the reverse procedure – building the novelette like a sonata-allegro.)

As Strauss grew older, his desire to overwhelm us with the musical equivalent of an epic novelist's entangled plot line abated; and as the tone poem period came to an end, he began to enjoy what was, at first, a coy flirtation with the *style gallant* and then to visit with increasing ardor the spirit of tonal rebirth and re-emphasis which dominated the preclassic generations. It has always seemed to me that the pivotal work in Strauss's career is one of the less spectacular, and certainly in North America least well known, of his works – *Ariadne auf Naxos. Ariadne* is neither the most brilliant, the most effective, nor the most likable of Strauss's operas, and yet from its conception date those qualities which can now be numbered as the outstanding traits of the mature composer. (There may be some amusement in the fact that this statement, however open to challenge, should be made of a work written in the same year as Stravinsky's *Sacre du printemps* and Schoenberg's *Pierrot Lunaire* – 1912.) *Ariadne* finally confirms what must surely have been suspected of Strauss long before – that at heart his instinct, if not neoclassic, is essentially that of a highly intellectualized romantic.

From *Ariadne* onward his textures will on the whole become ever more transparent, and the buoyancy and stability of his harmonic style will be even more magnificently served. Strauss always fancied himself as a kind of twentieth-century Mozart, and this is not an altogether insupportable conceit: indeed, in many of the operas of the middle-late years from *Ariadne* to *Die schweigsame Frau* we find again and again the delicious transparency which makes these works, in my view, the most valid outlet for the neo-classic instinct. And so, once again, Strauss's concern for the total preservation of tonality finds not only a sanctuary but a point of departure.

I do not want to suggest that Strauss's creative life did not at some time actually undergo that terrifying evaporation of inspiration which plagues the sub-conscience of all creative people. It has always seemed to me there was some justification for the concern expressed about his artistic future during the period immediately following the First World War. Certainly, the decade following the Great War was the least productive decade of Strauss's life, and his work at that time, while possessed as always of an enormous technical competence, cannot by any stretch of the imagination be regarded as equaling his earlier achievements. Strauss himself, of course (utilizing the composer's and the parent's privilege of making a special pet of the unwanted child), swore to his dying day that *Die Frau ohne Schatten* was the greatest of his operas and besieged major opera houses with requests for its production. He even insisted that, although his health could not possibly permit him to endure the rigours of conducting *Rosenkavalier* (because of its length), he would nonetheless be most happy to conduct *Frau ohne Schatten* (which is slightly longer). The middle operas like *Frau ohne Schatten* are certainly not without admirable qualities; we no longer feel, however, quite that same wondrous stroke of inevitability which in the earlier works – and, indeed, the later ones – bound the first note with the last and made all the ingenious technical diversions not the aim but simply, and rightly, the means.

And so we come to that incredible rejuvenation of Strauss the artist – the fluent, warm, infinitely moving works of his late years. Here, surely, is one of the most fascinating revitalizations of the creative spirit to which we could ever be witness. One could, I suppose, attempt a parallel with the last works of Beethoven by pointing to the fact that they too follow upon a dreary desert of inactivity, from which Beethoven emerged to find not only the assured step of his youth but, indeed, a means to express the mature deliberation of his later years. It is my view that the late works of Strauss afford much the same opportunity to contemplate the mating of a philosophic stance and a technical accomplishment indivisible from it. I feel that in virtually all of his late works Strauss's youthful tendency to celebrate through the techniques of art the human conquest of material order, to applaud the existential character who flings himself unquestioningly against the world – in other words to be the hero of *Ein Heldenleben* – is now sublimated, indeed, wholly vanquished, by a technical mastery which no longer needs to prove itself, to flaunt its virility – but which has become inseparable from those qualities of sublime resignation that are the ultimate achievements of great age and great wisdom.

Indeed, short of the last quartets of Beethoven, I can think of no music which more perfectly conveys that transfiguring light of ultimate philosophic repose than does *Metamorphosen* or *Capriccio* – both written when their composer was past seventy-five. In these late works the vast harmonic imagination always characteristic of Strauss remains; but whereas in the earlier years it had the positive, convinced, untroubled assurance of metric simplicity, now it is sometimes tentative, sometimes wayward, sometimes deliberately asymmetric, and thus conveys a vivid sense of one who has experienced great doubt and still finds affirmation, of one who has questioned the very act of creativity and found it good, of one who has recognized the many sides of truth.

And yet I wonder how vivid the comparison with Beethoven really is. Beethoven, after all, in the last quartets did virtually bridge the entire romantic era and afford a link with the taut motivic complexities of the Schoenbergian generation. On the other hand, at least from our present point of view, Strauss, in the later years, can hardly be supposed to have suggested any such stylistic o'erleaping of future generations. He has, if my view of him is substantial, simply brought to an inevitable and poignant conclusion his own existence as a creative man; he has promised nothing whatever for the future. And this, I submit, is where the estimation of my generation has passed Strauss by.

I do not for one minute suggest that, with all of my admiration for Richard Strauss, I could possibly imagine that the future of music will somehow be influenced in any actual, stylistic sense by his works. But then what is it that really provides the influence of one generation upon another? Is it simply the retention of stylistic similarities within an ever-moving historical front? Or can it not also be the inspiration to be drawn from a life which contains a total achievement of art? Certainly Richard Strauss had very little to do with the twentieth century as we know it. No more perhaps did he belong in the Age of the Atom than Sebastian Bach in the Age of Reason or Gesualdo in the High Renaissance.

By all the aesthetic and philosophic yardsticks that we must apply, he was not a man of our time. Can we really conceive of *Frau ohne Schatten* being launched in the inflation-ridden, ragtime-infested Roaring Twenties? Is it really possible that *Capriccio*, that autumnal salute to a world of gallant poise and quiet literacy, could really have been born while the flames of war swept our world of 1941?

The great thing about the music of Richard Strauss is that it presents and substantiates an argument which transcends all the dogmatisms of art – all questions of style and taste and idiom – all the frivolous, effete preoccupations of the chronologist. It presents to us an example of the man who makes richer his own time by not being of it; who speaks for all generations by being of none. It is an ultimate argument of individuality – an argument that man can create his own synthesis of time without being bound by the conformities that time imposes.

——•◆•——

Letter from Hugo von Hofmannsthal (librettist)
to Richard Strauss dated 8th March 1912:

Dear Dr. Strauss,

I have often felt that those of our subjects (Rosenkavalier, Ariadne, Die Frau ohne Schatten) *which treat of purification, of a Goethean atmosphere, and in which your profound understanding has given me infinite satisfaction – that all these subjects arouse aspects of your genius, the spiritual and the lovely, which, though hinted at in* Elektra *and* Salome, *are not seen there as an integral part of your equipment. These same subjects also arouse much that has an affinity with your Lieder, with* Don Quixote, *with* Eulenspiegel; *but at the same time they offer only small scope to other sides of your fecund nature – I mean to those massive, grandiose, wholly compelling qualities which chiefly distinguish you from every other living composer and give you a position without equal anywhere.*

HOWARDS END

E.M. Forster

IT WILL BE GENERALLY ADMITTED that Beethoven's Fifth Symphony
is the most sublime noise that has ever penetrated into the ear of
man. All sorts of conditions are satisfied by it. Whether you are like
Mrs Munt, and tap surreptitiously when the tunes come – of course,
not so as to disturb the others; or like Helen who can see heroes and
shipwrecks in the music's flood; or like Margaret, who can only see
the music; or like Tibby, who is profoundly versed in counterpoint,
and holds the full score open on his knee; or like their cousin,
Fräulein Mosebach, who remembers all the time that Beethoven is
'echt Deutsch'; or like Fräulein Mosebach's young man, who can
remember nothing but Fräulein Mosebach: in any case, the passion
of your life becomes more vivid, and you are bound to admit that
such a noise is cheap at two shillings. It is cheap, even if you hear it
in the Queen's Hall, dreariest music-room in London, though not as
dreary as the Free Trade Hall, Manchester; and even if you sit on the
extreme left of the that hall, so that the brass bumps at you before
the rest of the orchestra arrives, it is still cheap.

'Who is Margaret talking to?' said Mrs Munt, at the conclusion of
the first movement. She was again in London on a visit to Wickham
Place.

Helen looked down the long line of their party, and said that she
did not know.

'Would it be some young man or other whom she takes an interest
in?'

'The Box by the Stalls' by Jean Beraud (1849-1935), c.1883. Oil on canvas.

'I expect so,' Helen replied. Music enwrapped her, and she could not enter into the distinction that divides young men whom one takes an interest in from young men whom one knows.

'You girls are so wonderful in always having – oh dear! We mustn't talk.'

For the Andante had begun – very beautiful, but bearing a family likeness to all the other beautiful Andantes that Beethoven has written, and, to Helen's mind, rather disconnecting the heroes and shipwrecks of the first movement from the heroes and goblins of the third. She heard the tune through once, and then her attention wandered, and she gazed at the audience, or the organ, or the architecture. Much did she censure the attenuated Cupids who encircle the ceiling of the Queen's Hall, inclining each to each with vapid gesture, and clad in sallow pantaloons, on which the October sunlight struck. 'How awful to marry a man like those Cupids!' thought Helen. Here Beethoven started decorating his tune, so she heard him through once more, and then she smiled at her cousin Frieda. But Frieda, listening to Classical Music, could not respond. Herr Liesecke, too, looked as if wild horses could not make him inattentive; there were lines across his forehead, his lips were parted, his pince-nez at right angles to his nose, and he had laid a thick, white hand on either knee. And next to her was Aunt Juley, so British, and wanting to tap. How interesting that row of people was! What diverse influences had gone to their making! Here Beethoven, after humming and hawing with great sweetness, said 'Heigho' and the Andante came to an end. Applause, and a round of wunderschöning and prachtvolleying from the German contingent. Margaret started talking to her new young man; Helen said to her aunt: 'Now comes the wonderful movement: first of all the goblins, and then a trio of elephants dancing'; and Tibby implored the company generally to look out for the transitional passage on the drum.

'On the what, dear?'

Ludwig van Beethoven by Ferdinand Georg Waldmueller, 1823. Oil on canvas.

'On the *drum*, Aunt Juley.'

'No; look out for the part where you think you have done with the goblins and they come back,' breathed Helen, as the music started with a goblin walking quietly over the universe, from end to end. Others followed him. They were not aggressive creatures; it was that that made them so terrible to Helen. They merely observed in passing that there was no such thing as splendour or heroism in the world. After the interlude of elephants dancing, they returned and made the observation for the second time. Helen could not contradict them for, once at all events, she had felt the same, and had seen the reliable walls of youth collapse. Panic and emptiness! Panic and emptiness! The goblins were right.

Her brother raised his finger: it was the transitional passage of the drum.

For, as if things were going too far, Beethoven took hold of the goblins and made them do what he wanted. He appeared in person. He gave them a little push, and they began to walk in a major key instead of in a minor, and then – he blew with his mouth and they were scattered! Gusts of splendour, gods and demigods contending with vast swords, colour and fragrance broadcast on the field of battle, magnificent victory, magnificent death! Oh, it all burst before the girl, and she even stretched out her gloved hands as if it was tangible. Any fate was titanic; any contest desirable; conqueror and conquered would alike be applauded by the angels of the utmost stars.

And the goblins – they had not really been there at all? They were only the phantoms of cowardice and unbelief? One healthy human impulse would dispel them? Men like the Wilcoxes, or President Roosevelt, would say yes. Beethoven knew better. The goblins really had been there. They might return – and they did. It was as if the splendour of life might boil over and waste to stream and froth. In its dissolution one heard the terrible, ominous note, and a goblin, with increased malignity, walked quietly over the universe from end to end. Panic and emptiness! Panic and emptiness! Even the flaming ramparts of the world might fall.

Beethoven chose to make all right in the end. He built the ramparts up. He blew with his mouth for the second time, and again the goblins were scattered. He brought back the gusts of splendour, the heroism, the youth, the magnificence of life and of death, and, amid vast roarings of a superhuman joy, he led his Fifth Symphony to its conclusion. But the goblins were there. They could return. He had said so bravely, and that is why one can trust Beethoven when he says other things.

Helen pushed her way out during the applause. She desired to be alone. The music had summed up to her all that had happened or could happen in her career. She read it as a tangible statement, which could never be superseded. The notes meant this and that to her, and they could have no other meaning, and life could have no other meaning. She pushed right out of the building, and walked slowly down the outside staircase, breathing the autumnal air, and then she strolled home.

TRIO

Rohan de Saram

Rohan de Saram, of Sri Lankan origin, studied with Gaspar Cassado and Pablo Casals, performing as a soloist with major orchestras around the world. For many years he was the cellist of the Arditti Quartet. During his first years in England, living in Oxford, he stayed at the home of the Deneke sisters who were closely connected to the Schumann/Brahms circle of artists and composers. This gave him an unusual insight into 19th century European musical history.

DURING APPROXIMATELY twelve years of my life, from c.1958-1970, I lived in Oxford at "Gunfield", the home of Margaret and Helena Deneke. The house got its name from the fact that Oliver Cromwell had his army positioned there during the English Civil War. The parents of Marga and Lena, as they were called, had come to England during the 1870s from Germany. Both sisters were born and brought up in England but spoke German in the family. Music played a very important part in their lives and the first person to sign their visitors' book, which they left to me, was Clara Schumann, dated April 1894, and a few pages on are the signatures of Joseph Joachim and Robert Hausmann, the leader and cellist of the Joachim Quartet, both of whom were close friends of Brahms, who wrote his last orchestral work, the Double Concerto for violin, cello and orchestra, for them. Marga, herself a very good pianist, had been taught for some time by Eugenie Schumann, the youngest daughter of Robert and Clara Schumann.

As "Gunfield" was very much a 19th century style household, with

Robert and Clara Schumann in 1847 by Eduard Kaiser. Clara Schumann: German pianist and composer (1819-1896) married to Robert Schumann: German composer (1810-1856).

no television and only a rudimentary radio, our evenings were often spent playing the piano *à quatre mains*, getting to know the symphonies and chamber music repertoire. On some evenings I would go through the text of a Bach cantata, or some lieder by Schubert or Schumann, with Lena who taught German language and literature at Oxford University. One important fact I became aware of at this time was the transformation of the mainstream of music from the strongly Italian influenced style of Haydn, Mozart and early Beethoven to the equally strongly German influenced style of Wagner and Brahms. The latter two composers lived at a time when the rest of Europe was also inspired by waves of nationalism, Russia, Czechoslovakia, France, England and, a little later, Spain and Hungary, to name a few. In his paper *Neue Zeitschrift*, and in the early 1830s, Schumann, with his famous phrase, "Hats off, gentleman ... a genius", drew attention to Chopin, who among other things was certainly inspired by Polish dance forms such as the mazurka and polonaise. Schumann himself gave a large percentage of his playing instructions in German rather than Italian, whereas Brahms almost always used Italian, with the very occasional German translation. This small detail gives an insight into Brahms' possible mode of thinking: the language which served his illustrious predecessors, Bach, Haydn, Mozart and Beethoven, with the exception of an occasional use of German in his late works, would be sufficient for him. Schumann, on the other hand, had the *avant-garde* composer's interest in new forms, ideas and techniques, although he could also work in traditional forms, in which his instructions are generally in Italian.

Brahms, who it is said used to say that the two most important events in Germany during his lifetime were Bismarck's German unification and the Bach Gesellschaft, to which he personally contributed, must have been proud to be German, although he very much valued his visits to Italy and getting to know its great past.

Portrait of Johannes Brahms (1833-1897) by Josef Novak, 1860.

He would have been the first to appreciate the wider European interests of a composer like Bach, who used so many of the forms originating in Italy, France and the polyphonic music of the Netherlands some centuries before him. Some of his standardised suite forms were almost a symbol of a united Europe: the German allemande, the Italian or French courante or corrente, the Spanish sarabande, the French bourrée, gavotte or menuet, and the gigue from Ireland or England, not to mention the Polish polacca from the first Brandenburg Concerto.

The nationalistic focus during the 19th century in Europe produced some wonderful music, but at the same time certain interesting reactions, such as Tchaikovsky reportedly finding Brahms' music "dry and lacking beauty"; and even such a notable 20th century composer as Benjamin Britten, who was a great devotee of Tchaikovsky, is said to have expressed a dislike of Brahms' music. These are just two examples that come to mind, but over the years I have met many musicians as well as ordinary listeners who have found Brahms a "difficult" composer! This has puzzled me. I can only think that it has something to do with his "German" characteristics. One has to admit that in Germany's two major composers of the later 19th century, in Brahms and certainly in Wagner, the rhythmic/dance element is somewhat in abeyance in favour of the melodic/song element. In Germany after Bach's great synthesis in the middle of the 18th century (not dissimilar in many respects to the sophistication of harmony and polyphony at the end of the 19th century with Wagner and Brahms) music had a renewed "childhood", with great rhythmic vitality under Italian influence with C.P.E Bach, Haydn and Mozart, growing into a vigorous "manhood" of rhythmic vitality with denser instrumental textures with Beethoven, and a "middle age" with less purely rhythmic vitality and more harmonic/polyphonic sophistication with later Beethoven, Brahms and Wagner. Other European nations did not have this long and consistently great musical history and therefore showed the rhythmic vitality of younger musical cultures, where the national inspiration was often allied to a more adventurous sense of instrumental colour (Russian, Czech, French, to name a few) than German musical thinking demanded – with the possible exception of Richard Strauss. Schumann, never a virtuoso with orchestral colour, did however show a wide range of styles in his writing for the pianoforte: from the clear-textured and moving pieces of *Kinderszenen* to the deep and turbulent style of the great *Fantasie* opus 17 dedicated to Liszt. In this and other works of a similarly passionate *Leidenschaftlich* nature, Schumann required a style of pianoforte playing somewhat far removed from the clear textures of Mendelssohn and Chopin (of course with certain exceptions such as the short finale of the B flat minor Sonata, and a few other examples). It is well known how much Schumann appreciated both Mendelssohn and Chopin, although it is not known what either of them thought of this aspect of Schumann, breaking as it did traditional values which went back to Italian roots, and pointing to a future which would be taken up by Brahms. Between these two great figures* of German music was Clara Schumann, one of the great pianists of her time, the woman who was wife to one for sixteen years and closest friend to the other for over forty years, and the greatest inspiration to both. As Wagner and Liszt formed a trio with Cosima, Liszt's daughter and Wagner's wife, in the middle, so in this trio Schumann and Brahms had Clara in the middle. The two trios point to two different ideals of life.

---

* It is interesting to note that Schumann was twenty-three when Brahms was born and that Brahms was twenty-three when Schumann died.

DOCTOR FAUSTUS

Thomas Mann

In this twentieth-century version of the Faust legend, the life story of the great pioneering (and fictitious) composer Adrian Leverkühn is narrated by his faithful friend Serenus Zeitblom. Leverkühn will go on to make his own deranged, symbolic pact with the devil, as Germany makes its pact with Hitler, but in this extract the friends are theological students and Leverkühn is inspired by the magic of music through his German American lecturer Wendell Kretzschmar. Zeitblom writes about his animated conversations with Leverkühn.

IN SUCH TALK, with which he teased and irritated me, there was much that was merely imitative. But he had a way of adapting what he picked up and giving it a personal character which took from his adaptations anything that might sound ridiculous, if not everything boyish and derivative. He commented a good deal too – or we commented in lively exchange – on a lecture of Kretschmar's called "Music and the Eye" – likewise an offering which deserved a larger audience. As the title indicates, our lecturer spoke of his art in so far as – or rather, also as – it appeals to the sense of sight, which, so he developed his theme, it does in that one puts it down, through the notation, the tonal writing which – since the days of the old neumes, those arrangements of strokes and points, which had more or less indicated the flow of sound – had been practised with growing care and pains. His demonstration became very diverting, and likewise flattering, since it assumed in us a certain apprentice and brush-water

Portrait of Ludwig van Beethoven (1770-1827), holding the Missa Solemnis, by Joseph Karl Stieler (1781-1858), 1819.

intimacy with music. Many a turn of phrase in musician's jargon came not from the acoustic but the visual, the note-picture: for instance, one speaks of *occhiali* because the broken drum-basses, half notes that are coupled by a stroke through their necks, look like a pair of spectacles; or as one calls "cobbler's patches" (*rosalia*) certain cheap sequences one after another in stages at like intervals (he wrote examples for us on the blackboard). He spoke of the mere appearance of musical notation, and assured us that a knowledgeable person could get from one look at the notation a decisive impression of the spirit and value of a composition. Thus it had once happened to him that a colleague, visiting his room where an uninspired work submitted to him by a dilettante was spread out on the desk, had shouted: "Well, for heaven's sake, what sort of tripe is that you've got there?" On the other hand he sketched for us the enchanting pleasure which even the visual picture of a score by Mozart afforded to the practised eye; the clarity of the texture, the beautiful disposition of the instrumental groups, the ingenious and varied writing of the melodic line. A deaf man, he cried, quite ignorant of sound, could not but delight in these gracious visions. "To hear with eyes belongs to love's fine wit," he quoted from a Shakespeare sonnet, and asserted that in all time composers had secretly nested in their writings things that were meant more for the reading eye than for the ear. When, for instance, the Dutch masters of polyphony in their endless devices for the crossing of parts had so arranged them contrapuntally that one part had been like another when read backwards; that could not be perceived by the way they actually sounded, and he would wager that very few people would have detected the trick by ear, for it was intended rather for the eye of the guild. Thus Orlandus Lassus in the *Marriage at Cana* used six voices to represent the six water-jugs, which could be better perceived by seeing the music than by hearing it; and in the St. John Passion by Joachim von Burck "one of the servants," who gave Jesus a slap in the face, has only one note, but, on the "zween" (two) in the next phrase, "with him two others," there are two.

He produced several such Pythagorean jests, intended more for the eye than the ear, which music had now and again been pleased to make and came out roundly with the statement that in the last analysis he ascribed to the art a certain inborn lack of the sensuous, yes an anti-sensuality, a sacret tendency to asceticism. Music was actually the most intellectual of all the arts, as was evident from the fact that in it, as in no other, form and content are interwoven and absolutely one and the same. We say of course that music "addresses itself to the ear"; but it does so only in a qualified way, only in so far, namely, as the hearing, like the other senses, is the deputy, the instrument, and the receiver of the mind. Perhaps, said Kretschmar, it was music's deepest wish not to be heard at all, nor even seen, nor yet felt; but only – if that were possible – in some Beyond, the other side of sense and sentiment, to be perceived and contemplated as pure mind, pure spirit. But bound as she was to the world of sense, music must ever strive after the strongest, yes, the most seductive sensuous realization: she is a Kundry, who wills not what she does and flings soft arms of lust round the neck of the fool. Her most powerful realization for the senses she finds in orchestral music, where through the ear she seems to affect all the senses with her opiate wand and to mingle the pleasures of the realm of sound with those of colour and scent. Here, rightly, she was the penitent in the garb of the seductress. But there was an instrument – that is to say, a musical means of realization – through which music, while becoming audible to the sense of hearing, did so in a half-unsensuous, an almost abstract way, audible, that is, in a way peculiarly suited to its intellectual nature. He meant the piano, an instrument that is not an instrument at all in the sense of the others, since all specialization is foreign to it. It can, indeed, like them, be used in a solo performance and as a medium of virtuosity;

but that is the exceptional case and speaking very precisely a misuse. The piano, properly speaking, is the direct and sovereign representative of music itself in its intellectuality, and for that reason one must learn it. But piano lessons should not be – or not essentially and not first and last – lessons in a special ability, but lessons in m–m–

"Music!" cried a voice from the tiny audience, for the speaker could simply not get the word out, often as he had used it before, but kept on mumbling the *m*.

"Yes, of course," said he, released and relieved. Took a swallow of water and went his way.

But perhaps I may be pardoned for letting him appear once more. For I am concerned with a fourth lecture which he gave us, and I would have left out one of the others if necessary, rather than this, since no other – not to speak of myself – made such a deep impression on Adrian.

I cannot recollect its exact title. It was "The Elemental in Music" or "Music and the Elemental" or "The Elements of Music" or something like that. In any case the elemental, the primitive, the primeval beginning, played the chief role in it, as well as the idea that among all the arts it was precisely music that – whatever the richly complicated and finely developed and marvellous structure she had developed into in the course of the centuries – had never got rid of a religious attitude towards her own beginnings; a pious proneness to call them up in solemn invocation – in short, to celebrate her elements. She thus celebrates, he said, her cosmic aptitude for allegory; for those elements were, as it were, the first and simplest materials of the world, a parallelism of which a philosophizing artist of a day not long gone by – it was Wagner again of whom he spoke – had shrewdly, perhaps with somewhat too mechanical, too ingenious cleverness, made use, in that in his cosmogonic myth of the *Ring* he made the basic elements of music one with those of the world. To him the beginning of all things had its music, the E-flat major triad of the flowing depths of the Rhine, the seven primitive chords, out of which, as though out of blocks of Cyclopean masonry, primeval stone, the "Götterburg" arose. Surpassingly brilliant, in the grand style, he presented the mythology of music at the same time with that of the world; in that he bound the music to the things and made them express themselves in music, he created an apparatus of sensuous simultaneity – most magnificent and heavy with meaning, if a bit too clever after all, in comparison with certain revelations of the elemental in the art of the pure musicians, Beethoven and Bach; for example, in the prelude to the cello suite of the latter – also an E-flat major piece, built up in primitive triads. And he spoke of Anton Bruckner, who loved to refresh himself at the organ or piano by the simple succession of triads. "Is there anything more heartfelt, more glorious," he would cry, "than such a progression of mere triads? Is it not like a purifying bath for the mind?" This saying too, Kretschmar thought, was a piece of evidence worth thinking about, for the tendency of music to plunge back into the elemental and admire herself in her primitive beginnings.

Yes, the lecturer cried, it lay in the very nature of this singular art that it was at any moment capable of beginning at the beginning, of discovering itself afresh out of nothing, bare of all knowledge of its past cultural history, and of creating anew. It would then run through the same primitive stages as in its historical beginnings and could on one short course, apart from the main massif of its development, alone and unheeded by the world, reach most extraordinary and singular heights. And now he told us a story which in the most fantastic and suggestive way fitted into the frame of his present theme.

At about the middle of the eighteenth century there had flourished in his native home in Pennsylvania a German community of pious people belonging to the Baptist sect. Their leading and spiritually most respected members lived celibate lives and had therefore been honoured with the name of Solitary Brethren and Sisters; but the majority of them reconciled with the married state an exemplarily pure and godly manner of life, strictly regulated, hard-working and dietetically sound, full of sacrifice and self-discipline. Their settlements had been two: one called Ephrata, in Lancaster County, the other in Franklin County, called Snowhill; and they had looked up reverently to their head shepherd and spiritual father, the founder of the sect, a man named Beissel, in whose character fervent devotion to God mingled with the qualities of leadership, and fanatic religiosity with a lively and blunt-spoken energy.

Johann Conrad Beissel had been born of very poor parents at Eberbach in the Palatinate and early orphaned. He had learned the baker's trade and as a roving journeyman had made connections with Pietists and devotees of the Baptist confession, which had awakened in him slumbering inclinations towards an explicit service of the truth and a freely arising conviction of God. All this had brought him dangerously near to a sphere regarded in his country as heretical, and the thirty-year-old man decided to flee from the intolerance of the Old World and emigrate to America. There, in various places, in Germantown and Conestoga, he worked for a while as a weaver. Then a fresh impulse of religious devotion came over him and he had followed his inward voice, leading as a hermit in the wilderness an entirely solitary and meagre life, fixed only upon God. But as it will happen that flight from mankind sometimes only involves the more with humanity the man who flees, so Beissel had soon seen himself surrounded by a troop of admiring followers and imitators of his way of life, and instead of being free of the world, he had unexpectedly become, in the turning of a hand, the head of a community, which quickly developed into an independent sect, the Seventh-Day Anabaptists. He commanded them the more absolutely in that, so far as he knew, he had never sought the leadership, but was rather called to it against his intention and desire.

Beissel had never enjoyed any education worth mentioning, but in his awakened state he had mastered by himself the skills of reading and writing, and as his mind surged like the sea, tumultuous with mystical feelings and ideas, the result was that he filled his office chiefly as writer and poet and fed the souls of his flock: a stream of didactic prose and religious songs poured from his pen to the edification of his brethren in their silent hours and to the enrichment of their services. His style was high-flown and cryptic, laden with metaphor, obscure Scriptural allusions, and a sort of erotic symbolism. A tract on the Sabbath, *Mystyrion Anomalias,* and a collection of ninety-one *Mystical and Very Secret Sayings* were the beginning. A series of hymns followed on, which were to be sung to well-known European choral melodies, and appeared in print under such titles as *Songs for God's Love and Praise, Jacob's Place of Struggle and Elevation, Zionist Hill of Incense.* It was these little collections that a few years later, enlarged and improved, became the official song-book of the Seventh-Day Baptists of Ephrata, with the sweetly mournful title "Song of the Lonely and Forsaken Turtle Dove, The Christian Church." Printed and reprinted, further enriched by the emulative members of the sect, single and married, men and even more women, the standard work changed its title and also appeared once as *Miracle Play in Paradise.* It finally contained not less than seven hundred and seventy hymns, among them some with an enormous number of stanzas.

The songs were meant to be sung, but they lacked music. They were new texts to old tunes and were so used for years by the community. But now a new inspiration visited Johann Conrad Beissel. The spirit commanded him to take himself in addition to the role of poet and prophet that of composer.

There had been a young man staying at Ephrata, a young adept of the art of music, who held a singing-class; Beissel loved to attend and listen to the instruction. He must thus have made the discovery that music afforded possibilities for the extension and realization of the kingdom of the spirit, in a way of which young Herr Ludwig never dreamed. The extraordinary man's resolve was swiftly formed. No longer of the youngest, already far on in the fifties, he applied himself to work out a musical theory of his own, suited to his special requirements. He put the singing-teacher aside and took things firmly in his own hands – with such success that before long he had made music the most important element in the religious life of the community.

Most of the chorals, which had come over from Europe, seemed to him much too forced, complicated, and artificial to serve for his flock. He wanted to do something new and better and to inaugurate a music better answering to the simplicity of their souls and enabling them by practice to bring it to their own simple perfection. An ingenious and practical theory of melody was swiftly and boldly resolved on. He declared that there should be "master" and "servants" in every scale. Having decided to regard the common chord as the melodic centre of any given key, he called "masters" the notes belonging to this chord, and the rest of the scale "servants." And those syllables of a text upon which the accent lay had always to be presented by a "master," the unaccented by a "servant."

As for the harmony, he made use of a summary procedure. He made chord-tables for all possible keys, with the help of which anybody could write out his tunes comfortably enough, in four or five parts; and thus he caused a perfect rage for composition in the community. Soon there was no longer a single Seventh-Day Baptist, whether male or female, who, thus assisted, had not imitated the master and composed music.

Rhythm was now the part of theory which remained to be dealt with by this redoubtable man. He accomplished it with consummate success. He painstakingly followed with the music the cadence of the words, simply by providing the accented syllables with longer notes, and giving the unaccented shorter ones. To establish a fixed relation between the values of the notes did not occur to him; and just for that reason he preserved considerable flexibility for his metre. Like practically all the music of his time it was written in recurrent metres of like length – that is to say, in bars – but he either did not know this or did not trouble about it. This ignorance or unconcern, however, was above all else to his advantage; for the free, fluctuating rhythm made some of his compositions, particularly his setting of prose, extraordinarily effective.

This man cultivated the field of music, once he had entered it, with the same persistence with which he had pursued all of his other aims. He put together his thoughts on theory and published this as a preface to the book of the *Turtle Dove*. In uninterrupted application he provided with musical settings all the poems in the *Mount of Incense*, some of them with two or three, and set to music all the hymns he had himself ever written, as well as a great many by his pupils. Not satisfied with that, he wrote a number of more extended chorals, with texts taken direct from the Bible. It seemed as though he was about to set to music according to his own receipt the whole of the Scriptures; certainly he was the man to conceive such a plan. If it did not come to that it was only because he had to devote a large part of his time to the performance of what he had done, the training in execution and instruction in singing – and in this field he now achieved the simply extraordinary.

The music of Ephrata, Kretschmar told us, was too unusual, too amazing and arbitrary, to be taken over by the world outside, and hence it had sunk into practical oblivion when the sect of the German Seventh-Day Baptists ceased to flourish. But a faint legend had persisted down the years, sufficient in fact to make known how utterly peculiar and moving it had been. The tones coming from the choir had resembled delicate instrumental music and evoked an impression of heavenly mildness and piety in the hearer. The whole had been sung falsetto, and the singers had scarcely opened their mouths or moved their lips – with wonderful acoustic effect. The sound, that is, had thus been thrown up to the rather low ceiling of the hall, and it had seemed as though the notes, unlike any familiar to man, and in any case unlike any known church music, floated down thence and hovered angelically above the heads of the assemblage.

His own father, Kretschmar said, had often heard these sounds as a young man, and in his old age, when he talked to his family about it, his eyes had always filled with tears. He had spent a summer near Snowhill and on a Friday evening, the beginning of the Sabbath, had once ridden over as an onlooker at the house of worship of those pious folk. After that he had gone again and again: every Friday, as the sun set, driven by a restless urge, he had saddled his horse and ridden the three miles to listen. It had been quite indescribable, not to be compared with anything in this world. He had, so the elder Kretschmar had said, sat in English, French, and Italian opera houses; that had been music for the ear, but Beissel's rang deep down into the soul and was nothing more nor less than a foretaste of heaven.

"A great art," so our reporter said in closing, "which, as it were aloof from time and time's great course, could develop a little private history of this kind, and by forgotten side-paths lead to such exceptional beautitudes."

I recall as though it were yesterday how I went home with Adrian after this lecture. Although we did not talk much, we were unwilling to separate; and from his uncle's house, whither I accompanied him, he went back with me to the shop, and then I back with him to Parochialstrasse. Though of course we often did that. We both made merry over the man Beissel, this backwoods dictator with his droll thirst for action, and agreed that his music reform reminded us very much of the passage in Terence: "to behave stupidly with reason." But Adrian's attitude to the curious phenomenon differed from mine in what was after all so distinctive a way that it soon occupied me more than the subject itself. I mean that even while he mocked he set store by preserving the right to appreciate; set store by the right, not to say the privilege of keeping a distance, which includes in itself the possibility of good-natured acceptance, of conditioned agreement, half-admiration, along with the mockery and laughter. Quite generally this claim to ironic remoteness, to an objectivity which surely is paying less honour to the thing than to the freedom of the person, has always seemed to me a sign of uncommon arrogance. In so young a person as Adrian then was, the presumption of this attitude, it must be admitted, is disquieting; it was calculated to cause one concern for the health of his soul. Of course it is also very impressive to a companion with a simpler mental constitution, and since I loved him, I loved his arrogance as well – perhaps I loved him for its sake. Yes, that is how it was: this arrogance was the chief motive of the fearful love which all my life I cherished for him in my heart.

"Leave me alone," said he, as with our hands in our overcoat pockets we went to and fro between our two dwellings, in the wintry mist that wrapped the gas-lamps, "leave me in peace with my old codger, I can do with him. At least he had a sense of order, and even a silly order is better than none at all."

"Surely," I answered him, "you won't defend such a ridiculous and dogmatic arrangement, such childish rationalism as this invention of masters and servants. Imagine how these Beissel hymns must have sounded, in which every accented syllable had to have one note of the chord fall on it!"

"In any case not sentimental," he responded, "rather rigidly conforming to the law, and that I approve. You can console yourself that there was plenty of play for the fancy you put high above the law, in the free use of the servant notes."

He had to laugh at the word, bent over as we walked, and laughed down upon the wet pavement.

"Funny, it's very funny," he said. "But one thing you will admit. Law, every law, has a chilling effect, and music has so much warmth anyhow, stable warmth, cow warmth, I'd like to say, that she can stand all sorts of regulated cooling off – she has even asked for it."

"There may be some truth in that," I admitted. "But our Beissel isn't after all any very striking example of it. You forget that his rhythm, quite unregulated and abandoned to feeling, at least balanced the rigidity of his melody. And then he invented a singing style for himself – up to the ceiling and then floating down in a seraphic falsetto – it must have been simply ravishing and certainly gave back to music all the bovine warmth that it had previously taken away through the pedantic cooling off."

"Ascetic, Kretschmar would say," he answered, "the ascetic cooling off. In that Father Beissel was very genuine. Music always does penance in advance for her retreat into the sensual. The old Dutchman made her do the rummest sort of tricks, to the glory of God; and it went harder and harder on her from all one hears, with no sense of appeal, excogitated by pure calculation. But then they had these penitential practices sung, delivered over to the sounding breath of the human voice, which is certainly the most stable-warm imaginable thing in the world of sound … ."

"You think so?"

"Why not? No unorganic instrumental sound can be compared with it. Abstract it may be, the human voice – the abstract human being, if you like. But that is a kind of abstraction more like that of the naked body – it is after all more a pudendum." I was silent, confounded. My thoughts took me far back in our, in his past.

"There you have it," said he, "your music." I was annoyed at the way he put it, it sounded like shoving music off on me, as though it were more my affair than his. "There you have the whole thing, she was always like that. Her strictness, or whatever you like to call the moralism of her form, must stand for an excuse for the ravishments of her actual sounds."

For a moment I felt myself the older, more mature.

"A gift of life like music," I responded, "not to say a gift of God, one ought not to explain by mocking antinomies, which only bear witness to the fullness of her nature. One must love her."

"Do you consider love the strongest emotion?" he asked.

"Do you know a stronger?"

"Yes, interest."

"By which you presumably mean a love from which the animal warmth has been withdrawn."

"Let us agree on the definition!" he laughed. "Good night!"

We had got back to the Leverkühn house, and he opened his door.

AN OPUS II

Robert Schumann

Robert Schumann was not only a great composer, he was also an influential critic and reviewer. His very first review, written when he was just 22 years old, was published in Allgemeine Musikalische Zeitung *on 7 December 1831.*

It included some classic observations about Chopin's Variations in B flat major, Op. 2. *In the review Schumann used imaginary characters, Florestan, Eusebius and Master Raro, to represent different aspects of his own nature. The narrator, Julius, is the pianist Julius Knorr. In this review Schumann also coined the famous phrase, 'Gentleman hats off, [here is] a genius.' Although Chopin did not fully agree with Schumann's interpretation of his piece, they maintained a friendship over many years.*

This recent translation from the German shows how vibrant and thought-provoking a writer Schumann was at this very early stage of his career.

THE OTHER DAY Eusebius stepped quietly through the door. You know the ironic smile on his pallid face, the one with which he tries to excite you. I was sitting with Florestan at the piano. Florestan is, as you know, one of those rare musicians who has long since predicted anything futuristic, new or strange; in the blink of an eye, the strange is no longer strange to them; the extraordinary immediately becomes their property. Eusebius, on the other hand, as lyrical as he is serene, plucks one flower at a time; he attaches himself with more difficulty, but more firmly, takes pleasure more rarely, but also more thoroughly and for longer; his studies are stricter and his piano performances more level-headed, but also more tender and technically accomplished than those of Florestan. With the words: "Hats off, gentlemen, a genius," Eusebius laid out a piece of music that we easily recognised as a movement from the Haslinger Odeon. We were not allowed to look at the title. I leafed absent-mindedly through the pages; this veiled enjoyment of soundless music was somewhat magical. Moreover, it occurred to me that every composer has his own individual way of arranging the notes visually: Beethoven looks different on paper to Mozart, in the same way that Jean Paul's prose differs from Goethe's. But here I felt as though I were being gazed at by strange, wondering eyes, the eyes of flowers, of basilisks, of peacocks, of maidens. At some points it became more lucid – I thought I could see Mozart's "La ci darem la mano" entwined through a hundred chords, Leporello seemed to blink at me and Don Giovanni flew past me in a white cloak. "Now play it," Florestan said to Eusebius, laughing, "we will keep our eyes shut and not disturb you." Eusebius obliged; squashed into a window recess, we listened. Eusebius played as if possessed, bringing countless characters to life most vividly; it was as though the spirit of the moment was lifting his fingers beyond their mechanical functions. Admittedly, Florestan's approval, with the exception of a peaceful smile, consisted of nothing more than a remark that the variations could have been written by Beethoven or Franz Schubert, had they been piano virtuosos. But when he turned to the title page and read simply: *La ci darem la mano*, variations for pianoforte by Frederic Chopin, Opus 2, and we both exclaimed astonished, "An Opus Two!" and Eusebius added: Vienna, published by Haslinger; and, as our faces glowed appreciably with great astonishment, little could be heard apart from a number of exclamations: "At last, something decent – Chopin – I have never heard the name – who could

Frederic Chopin. Spain, Mallorca, Royal Carthusian Monastery.

he be? – in any case – a genius – isn't that Zerlina laughing, or even
Leporello?" … there ensued a truly indescribable scene. Heated with
wine, Chopin and banter, we went off to Master Raro, who laughed
a lot and showed little interest in Opus Two: "Because I know you
and your new-fangled enthusiasm for Herz and Hünten – but why
not bring the Chopin round here?" We promised to do so the following day. Eusebius soon quietly bade good night: I stayed for a while
with Master Raro; Florestan, who for some time has had no home
of his own, raced through the moonlit alleyways to my house. At
midnight I found him in my sitting room, lying on the couch with his
eyes closed. "Chopin's *Variations*," he began sleepily, "are still going
round in my head: the whole thing is certainly dramatic and sufficiently Chopinesque," he continued, "although I found Eusebius'
rendition lacking in Paganinian execution and Fieldish attack; the
introduction, being so self-contained – (can you recall Leporello's
skips in thirds?) – does not seem to fit very well with the whole; but
the theme – (but why has he written it in *B* flat?) – the variations, the
final movement and the Adagio, are admittedly more than enough –
genius stares you in the face from every bar. Of course, dear Julius,
Don Giovanni, Zerlina, Leporello and Masetto are the speaking
characters (not including the chorus) – Zerlina's response in the
theme shows plenty of amorousness, the first variation could
perhaps be described as noble and coquettish – the Spanish lord
flirting most amiably with the peasant girl. However, this becomes
quite apparent in the second, which is much more intimate, more
comical, more quarrelsome, just like when two lovers try to catch
one another and laugh more than usual. But how everything changes
in the third! This one is full of moonlight and fairy magic, I tell you;
Masetto is standing at a distance, cursing audibly, for sure, although
it doesn't bother Don Giovanni much. – But the fourth, what do you
make of that, Julius? – (Eusebius played it in a very straight manner)
– doesn't it bounce like a bold, cheeky girl running towards her man,

although the Adagio (it seems very natural to me that Chopin repeats the first part) is in B flat minor, which could not be more appropriate, as its opening is a kind of moral admonition to Don Giovanni – it's wicked of course, but beautiful, that Leporello is eavesdropping behind the bushes, laughing and jeering, and that the oboes and clarinets ooze with magical enticement and that the blossoming B flat major should signify the first kiss of love. But all that is nothing compared to the last movement – do you have any wine left, Julius? – that is the whole Mozart finale – full of popping champagne corks (the whole thing is Champagne), clinking bottles – Leporello's voice in between, then the snatching, chasing spirits, the fleeing Don Giovanni – and finally the bold ending that calms beautifully and truly concludes it all. Florestan ended by saying that he had only ever experienced a similar feeling in Switzerland. When at the end of a beautiful day the evening sunlight, red and pink, climbs up to the glacial peaks before it *flutters away* and disappears, all mountains and valleys are filled with a gentle scent while the glacier stands calm, cold and firm, like a giant woken from his dreams. – "But now you should also awake to new dreams, Julius, and sleep!" – "My dear Florestan," I answered, "all of these private feelings may be praiseworthy because they are colourful; but no matter how subjective they may be and how little intention Chopin had of becoming a genius, I bow my head to his skill, his steady striving, his diligence and his imagination." Upon which we fell asleep.

CODA

Glenn Gould in conversation with Tim Page

TIM PAGE: Glenn, it's now about seventeen years since you left the concert stage. I'm not going to ask you why you left or whether you will return, both questions that you have answered eloquently on a number of occasions. But when you quit the stage, you stated rather unequivocally that the live concert was dead, period, and that recordings were the future of music. Since 1964, however, we have seen a tremendous resurgence of interest in the concert hall – the success of such endeavours as New York's Mostly Mozart Festival is a good example – while the recording industry is in serious trouble. Any second thoughts on this subject?

GLENN GOULD: Well, I did give myself the hedge of saying that concerts would die out by the year 2000, didn't I? We still have nineteen years to go, and by that time I will be too old to be bothered giving interviews [laughs], and I won't have to be responsible for my bad prognosis! As to the recording industry being in trouble, I remain optimistic. I suspect this is a cyclical thing; recording is not really in trouble in those countries where classical music means a great deal – in Germany, for example. This trouble is, to a large extent, North American; it's been coming on quite gradually for a number of years now, and it may or may not reverse itself. If it does not, it simply means that Americans are not terribly interested in classical music.

On the other hand, it doesn't seem as though the concert is going away as fast as I rather hoped it would ... for the good of all

Portrait of Glenn Gould by John F. Ross, 2008. Oil on canvas.

mankind. It has, however, changed. I haven't been to a concert since 1967, when, under considerable pressure, I attended a friend's recital. But I get the impression that a great many contemporary concerts are like reincarnated versions of the kinds of shows that Hans von Bülow did in Toronto a hundred years ago, when he played Beethoven's "Appassionata" Sonata immediately following a trained-horse act!

TP: A sort of contemporary vaudeville?

GG: Exactly! There is a return to the "trained-horse act" type of concert where a bit of this is followed with a bit of that and then a bit of something else – which I think is actually very nice. Twenty years ago there were very few flexible chamber concerts; you had a string quartet playing Beethoven or whatever, but there was no intermingling of interchangeable modules as now exists. That's all changed; I don't know if this is a sign of desperation – that the solo act can't sustain an entire evening anymore – or simply a more imaginative way of thinking, or possibly even a complete return to the musical thought of the 1880s. I'm not sure what significance this all has.

TP: I know you have a dim view of concerts in general. You once told the *New York Times* that you found all the live arts "immoral" because "one should not voyeuristically watch one's fellow human beings in testing situations that do not pragmatically need to be tested."

GG: Yes, I confess that I have always had grave misgivings about the motives of people who go to concerts, live theatre, whatever. I don't want to be unfair about this; in the past, I have sometimes made rather sweeping generalizations to the effect that anybody who attends a concert is a voyeur at the very best, and maybe a sadist to boot! I'm sure that this is not altogether true; there may even be people who prefer the acoustics in Avery Fisher Hall to those in their living room. So I don't want to be uncharitable. But

I do think that the whole business about asking people to test themselves in situations which have no need of their particular exertions is wrong – as well as pointless and cruel.

I'm afraid that the "Let's climb Everest just because it is there" syndrome cuts very little ice with me … there's a pun in there someplace. It makes no sense to do things that are difficult just to prove they can be done. Why climb mountains, or ski back down or dive out of airplanes or race motor cars, unless there is a manifest need for such behaviour?

The concert has been *replaced*, you know. I don't want to bore you with all the reasons why I think technology has superseded the concert – I've enumerated them on many other occasions, and I don't want to do that act again. But there is one reason which I think bears on this question: technology has the capability to create a climate of anonymity and to allow the artist the time and the freedom to prepare his conception of a work to the best of his ability, to perfect a statement without having to worry about trivia like nerves and finger slips. It has the capability of replacing those awful and degrading and humanly damaging uncertainties which the concert brings with it: it takes the specific personal performance information out of the musical experience. Whether the performer is going to climb the musical Everest on the particular occasion no longer matters. And it's for that reason that the word "immoral" comes into the picture. It's a difficult area – one where aesthetics touch upon theology, really – but I think that to have technology's capability and not to take advantage of it and create a contemplative climate if you can – *that* is immoral!

TP: When I said the recording industry was in trouble, I was perhaps thinking too much of economics, for in a strictly artistic sense it is certainly alive and well. In recent days there have been recordings of much formerly obscure material – early Haydn symphonies, Schubert operas, lesser know Bach cantatas – which went unheard for many years. And a lot of new works have been recorded. Let's talk about your repertoire. While you have recorded a fair amount of the standard literature – Bach, Beethoven, Mozart etc. – you have avoided recording some of the standard piano composers. For instance, do you think you will ever make a Chopin record?

GG: No. I don't think he is a very good composer. I played Op. 58 when I was younger, just to see how it would feel. It didn't feel very good, so I've never bothered to play any more Chopin.

I have always felt that the whole center core of the piano recital repertoire is a *colossal* waste of time. The whole first half of the nineteenth century – excluding Beethoven to some degree – is pretty much of a washout as far as solo instrumental music is concerned. This generalization includes Chopin, Liszt, Schumann – I'm tempted not to say Mendelssohn, because I have tremendous affection for his choral and chamber works, but most of his piano writing is pretty bad. You see, I don't think any of the early romantic composers knew how to write for the piano. Oh, they knew how to use the pedal, and how to make dramatic effects, splashing notes in every direction, but there's very little real *composing* going on. The music of that era is full of empty theatrical gestures, full of exhibitionism, and it has a worldly, hedonistic quality that simply turns me off.

Another problem as I see it is that Chopin, Schumann, and company labored under the delusion that the piano is a homophobic instrument. I don't think that's true; I think the piano is a contrapuntal instrument and only becomes interesting when it is treated in a manner in which the vertical and horizontal dimensions are mated. This does not happen in most of the material written for it in the first half of the nineteenth century.

In the late romantic period lies the big tragedy, for the composers in that period – Wagner, Richard Strauss, possibly Mahler – those composers who could have written with a tremendous

An 18th-century German portrait of composer and organist
Johann Sebastian Bach (Eisenach, 1685-Leipzig, 1750). Oil.

penetration of the intermingling of harmonic and thematic language just basically chose not to write for the piano at all. Wagner wrote an early sonata, but it makes Weber look like one of the great masters of all time by comparison. I suspect that Wagner had no real understanding of the piano, for the accompaniments to the *Wesendonk Lieder*, which are fine in their orchestral arrangement, don't work well on the piano at all. I transcribed and recorded a few of Wagner's large orchestral pieces some years back. It was a real labor of love. I simply wanted to have something of Wagner's I could play.

On the other hand, I have been recording the early Richard Strauss piano works – Op. 3, Op. 5, pieces Strauss wrote when he was sixteen – and they are minor miracles: as refined, as polished, as anything Mendelssohn did in his teen-age years. And with the exception of Mendelssohn, no sixteen-year-old has *ever* written with such craft and assurance – I am *not* forgetting Mozart. Strauss could write superbly for the piano – in the *Burleske*, in *Le Bourgeois Gentilhomme*, and particularly in the later songs, such as the *Ophelia Lieder*, which I recorded with Elisabeth Schwarzkopf. His piano writing is devoid of any ostentation, any exhibitionism or fake virtuosity. But he didn't choose to do much work in that genre.

That is the great pity – this gap in the piano repertoire. It was an orchestral period and the piano was little more than a backup, a poor man's orchestra, a substitute, "first draft" kind of instrument.

TP: The only piano piece by Strauss that comes easily to my mind is that little "Traumerei" that used to be included in those Theodore Presser-type "Great Musical Pieces for Piano" collections that were so prevalent at the turn of the century.

GG: I'll bet that's from Op. 9, which I haven't played yet. I've played Op. 3, which consists of sturdy little pieces in the intermezzo style.

None of the Op. 3 pieces have names, but all those in Op. 9 do. They're generally weaker pieces than those in Op. 3.

TP: My vision of Strauss is an unconventional one. Although he is often thought of as the late romantic par excellence, my favourite Strauss pieces are those from his old age, from his last period. I love the serene, nostalgic, and ultimately classical purity of such works as *Daphne*, *Capriccio*, and *Metamorphosen*.

GG: Do you know the writer Jonathan Cott? A very interesting man, and a friend of mine. We've actually never met; our relationship is ... terribly telephonic. Jonathan is a devoted, *fanatic* Straussian of the most lyrical order, and he speaks with the same reverence and enthusiasm that you do for works like *Metamorphosen*, *Capriccio*, and the Oboe Concerto.

It's interesting: when I made a documentary about Strauss last year, I got a strong response for the last pieces from a number of the younger people I talked with ... Jonathan Cott and the composer Stanley Silverman, for example. Silverman has considerable reservations about Strauss as an opera man but, again, loves the late works. It's the elder statesmen – like Norman Del Mar, who wrote the three-volume study of Strauss – who don't think so highly of the last pieces; but then you have a young man like Jonathan going on in an ecstatic way. Extraordinary – quite the reverse of the generation gap one would expect.

TP: There *is* a decline in Strauss's middle period.

GG: Oh, no question. I've never been able to take a work like *Ariadne* seriously – in fact, I'm not fond of *Der Rosenkavalier*. But even a work like the *Alpine* Symphony ... now this is a work which has had a very bad press all its life, but there are *moments* in that piece – even though, yes, the coda *does* go on forever, and no, he doesn't seem to know how to get off that pedal point at the end [*laughs*] – but there are those moments – indeed, great long swathes – that put to shame even the best of the early tone poems.

It doesn't hold together structurally in the way that something like *Till Eulenspiegel* does, but there is a seriousness of intent that simply wasn't there in the early years. And then pieces like *Capriccio!* I don't know *Daphne* that well; now that you mention it, I will have to study it.

TP: It's gorgeous. You can pass up the opera *Friedenstag*, however.

GG: Yes, I have a score of *that* one! [laughs] You know, Strauss was a much more abstract thinker than most people give him credit for, and the only romantic composer after Mendelssohn who never violated the integrity of which I might call the *inferential* bass of the voice-leading components in the structure of the music. (Some people would put in a claim for Brahms on that score, but he does slip up occasionally, and the rest of the time he's so *bloody* self-righteous about *not* slipping up.) *Metamorphosen* is my favourite Strauss piece, because in it he has finally come to terms with the abstract nature of his own gift. In a way, it's Strauss's *Art of the Fugue*. It's an *asexual* work, if you like, a work that has no gender. It could belong to the organ, or to the human voice, just as easily as to the twenty-three solo strings for which it was written. But anyway, I wandered off the point, because I started to say that it was a great shame that Richard Strauss did not write more for the piano. But I can tell you right now that I'm not going to help him out by transcribing *Metamorphosen*, because I haven't got that many fingers!

TP: Sibelius is also considered to be a late romantic, but once you get past the first couple of symphonies, there are few more austere and classical composers. You have recorded some of the piano music, which is all but unknown today.

GG: Yes, if you count little pieces within opus numbers – titles like "Traumerei" or "To a Fir Tree" [laughs] or whatever – Sibelius wrote something like a hundred and seventeen pieces for the piano. Most of them are completely insignificant, but I am fascinated by the three sonatines I recorded. They have the same Spartan concision, bordering on the stingy, that is found in his symphonies, but their idiom is almost neoclassical. Quite extraordinary, considering those sonatines predate World War I, yet they contain an anticipation of the postwar zeitgeist. But of course they are not masterpieces; nothing Sibelius wrote for the piano really was. He was mainly interested in the orchestra. I *do* admire the fact that when he does write for the piano, he doesn't attempt to make it into a surrogate orchestra. It is always definitely piano writing.

TP: I can understand how the Nordic music of Sibelius must appeal to you, for your interest in the far north is well known. You have made a radio docudrama entitled "The Idea of North," and I seem to remember that you once said something to the effect that it was difficult to go far north without becoming a philosopher.

GG: What I actually said was that most people I have met who actually did immerse themselves in the north seemed to end up, in whatever disorganized fashion, *being* philosophers. These people I met were government officials, university professors, and so on – people who had been very much exposed to a kind of unifying atmosphere. None of them were born in the north; they all *chose* to live there, for one reason or another. Whatever their motive in moving north may have been – and it varied from person to person – each individual seemed to go through a particular process which greatly altered his life.

At first, most of these people resisted the change: they reached out, contacted friends, made sure their subscription to *The New Yorker* was intact, and so on. But after a while they usually reached a point when they said to themselves: "No, that's *not* what I came up here to do."

In general, I found that the characters who had stuck it out long enough and removed themselves from the sense of curiosity about what their colleagues were thinking, or how the world reacted to what they had done, developed in an extraordinary way and underwent an extreme metamorphosis.

But I think that this can be true of anybody who chooses to live in an isolated way – even in the heart of Manhattan. I don't think the actual latitudinal factor is important at all. I chose "north" as a handy metaphor. It may be that the north is sometimes capable of providing a helping hand in getting people out of a situation they couldn't pry themselves loose from otherwise; it may be that looking at endless flowers on the tundra during the two procreative weeks in July is inspiring, but I don't think that the latitude is what made these people philosophers – if indeed that is what they became. No, it was this sense of saying, "I don't really *care* what my colleagues back at the University of Fill-in-the-Blank or at the department of external affairs think about this solitude, for *I* am going to do it, and *I* am going to discover something!"

TP: A purification process.

GG: Yes. This process could have occurred even had these people simply locked themselves in their closets ... although that might have been rather less attractive visually.

TP: So you really mean the disembodied "idea" of north.

GG: Precisely.

TP: In your docudramas you often use a technique where three or more voices are all talking at the same time, making it very difficult to zero in on any single sentence or idea. You have referred to this as "contrapuntal radio."

GG: Yes. I don't honestly believe that it is essential in radio that every word is heard. One emphasizes just enough key words in the ... countersubject sentences, if you will, so that the audience knows that voice is still happening, but it still allows them to zero in on the primary voice or voices and to treat the others as a sort of basso continuo.

We come from a long and splendid tradition of radio, but it has always been a tradition that was very, very linear. One person spoke, then the next person spoke, and occasionally they interrupted one another with an "and" or a "but". Two people never spoke together; that made no sense. I grew up in that particular tradition and enjoyed its products hugely. Nevertheless, I always felt that there was a musical dimension in the spoken word which was being totally ignored.

I coined the term "contrapuntal radio" to respond to certain criticism. When "The Idea of North" first came out in 1967, the fashionable word was "aleatory," and some critics were quick to apply this term to my work. *Nothing* could have been further from the truth, and to counter this impression, I began to speak of "contrapuntal radio," implying a highly organized discipline – not necessarily leading to a fugue in every incident, but in which every voice leads its own rather splendid life and adheres to certain parameters of harmonic discipline. I kept a very close ear as to how the voices came together and in what manner they splashed off each other, both in the actual sound and in the meaning of what was being said.

Now I am drafting an idea that I don't really expect to get to work on for a year or so, but at that point I intend to do a radio equivalent of Tallis's sixty-four-voice motet [laughs] – but I don't intend to say anything more about that, as it will probably jinx the whole project if I do!

TP: You have also worked with some of the same ideas in television.

GG: Yes, I've written a television script on the fugue, part of a series of five programs on Bach that I am doing for a German company. I've been having a really hard time with this project, because the rough guidelines are for forty minutes of music and only twenty minutes of talk. It is an absolutely impossible task to try to deliver any important thoughts on the nature of a fugue in twenty minutes.

There is nothing aleatoric about my television work, either. In the film, there is a discussion between myself and the director which will appear to be spontaneous. In reality, it will be the product of months of hard work, concise scripting, and rehearsal.

TP: Turning back to your piano recordings, I'd like to talk about your oft-quoted statement to the effect that the only excuse for recording a work is to do it differently.

GG: That's true, but I've always meant to immediately interject that *if*, however, that difference has nothing of validity to recommend it musically or organically, then better not record the work at all.

I am not without stain in this regard, because there are works that I have recorded simply for the sake of completeness that I had no convictions about whatsoever.

TP: Would this include some of Mozart's piano music? Your performances of some of the sonatas strike me as possibly your least successful records.

GG: Yes, a couple of the later Mozart sonatas. The early works I love, the middle ones I love, the later sonatas I do *not* like. I find them intolerable, loaded with a quasitheatrical conceit, and I can only say that I went about recording a piece like the Sonata in B-flat major, K. 570, with no more conviction whatsoever. The honest thing to do would have been to skip those works entirely, but the cycle had to be completed.

TP: You're not very enthusiastic about much of Beethoven's work, either.

GG: I have very ambivalent feelings about Beethoven. I'm absolutely at a loss for any reasonable explanation as to why his best known works – the Fifth Symphony, The Violin Concerto, the "Emperor," the "Waldstein" – ever became popular, much less as to why they have retained their appeal. Almost every criterion that I expect to encounter in great music – harmonic and rhythmic variety, contrapuntal invention – is almost entirely absent in these pieces. In his

Portrait of Wolfgang Amadeus Mozart (Salzburg, 1756-Vienna, 1791), Austrian composer and pianist. 18th-century Austrian painting.

middle period – the period which produced those works – Beethoven offered us the supreme historical example of a composer on an ego trip, a composer absolutely confident that whatever he did was justified simply because he did it! I don't know any other way to explain the predominance of those empty, banal, belligerent gestures that serve as his themes in that middle period. The later years are another story – my favourite Beethoven symphony is the Eighth, my favourite movement in all of his sonatas the opening of Op. 101, and, for me, the "Grosse Fuge" is not only the greatest work Beethoven ever wrote but just about the most astonishing piece in musical literature. But even the late works are remarkably inconsistent – for instance, I don't think that the remainder of Op. 101 has much to do with the extraordinary first movement, except for that quotation right before the finale.

All in all, I'd have to say that Beethoven's most consistently excellent works are those from his early period, before his hearing started to go – let's face it, that *did* affect his later work – and before his ego took complete command. Almost all of those early piano works are immaculately balanced – top to bottom, register to register. In these pieces, Beethoven's sense of structure, fantasy, variety, thematic continuity, harmonic propulsion, and contrapuntal discipline were absolutely, *miraculously* in alignment. I'm talking about the Sonatas Op. 26 and 28, and the variations like that marvellous set in Op. 34. These works have such a sense of peace, such a wonderful pastoral radiance, and every texture is as carefully worked out as it would be in a string quartet. What I'm going to say may surprise you – musicians are supposed to have more sophisticated tastes than this – but I think that one of Beethoven's real masterpieces is the "Moonlight" Sonata.

But even in these early years, I have to tell you that Mr. Beethoven and I do not see eye to eye on what constitutes good music. About 1801, Beethoven wrote a letter in which he stated that his best piano sonata to date was Op. 22. And much as I love the early sonatas – and I really *do* love them – there is one dud in the batch … and that is Op. 22.

TP: Do you think it is time for a return to epic forms? Many artists seem to believe this is what will be occurring in the next decade.

GG: I try to avoid thinking in such generalizations about musical/artistic trends. If I said, "Yes, it is time for the return of the epic," that would imply that there was some point in the past when it was *not* right to produce one. And I don't think that that is necessarily so.

Let's look at the year 1913 – no, no, 1912, even better. You have Arnold Schoenberg writing *Pierrot Lunaire*; Webern is working on the short pieces that immediately follow his string quartet miniatures, and Berg is composing the *Altenberg Lieder*. If the world stopped at this point, a historian would have to say, "The Age of the Epic is over; we are now in an age of fragmentation and the breakdown of the idea of the great long-breathed line of continuity in music." I simply *cannot* believe that this would be an adequate summation of the year 1912 – even though many music historians would describe its prevailing tendencies in this way. But at the same time Jan Sibelius was working on the first draft of his Fifth Symphony, which is certainly closer to epic than fragment! I don't think I need go any further than to point out the complete underlying absurdity of such generalizations.

I find it very disturbing to contemplate the lemminglike tendencies that artists in general assume – you know: the *anti*hero is in this year, the hero will be back next year. It shouldn't matter; one should be free of all that.

TP: Along the same lines, what would you say are the important issues confronting a composer in 1980?

GG: *Well* … I don't really know. I am unable to react to a situation in which a zeitgeist-compelled tendency suggests that a particular motivation is adequate or appropriate for more than one individual at a time. I would like to see a world where nobody cared what anybody else was doing – in which the entire group-think "You hold a C-major chord for thirty minutes, I'll hold it for thirty-one" syndrome utterly disappeared. This is not entirely a contemporary problem – twenty years ago, it manifested itself in a different way.

For this reason, I don't have an axe to grind. I can't say, "I would like to see the reaffirmation of the tonal system in all its original glory," or "I would like to see a return to pure Babbitt serialism, circa 1959." What I *would* like to see is a situation in which the particular pressures and polarizations that those systems have engendered among their adherents and their opponents just didn't exist.

I would think that the New York music scene would be a terribly difficult thing to be involved with unless one simply lived there and was quite specifically *not* a part of it. I find it very depressing to hear about situations in which this very competitive/imitative notion of what is au courant rules creativity. I can't think of anything *less* important.

One of the things I find most moving about the final Contrapunctus in *The Art of the Fugue* is that Bach was writing this music against *every possible tendency* of the time. He had renounced the kinds of modulatory patters that he himself had used successfully six or seven years earlier in the "Goldberg" Variations and in book 2 of *The Well-Tempered Clavier* and was writing in a lighter, less clearly defined early-baroque/late-Renaissance manner. It was as though he was saying to the world, "I don't *care* anymore; there are no more Italian Concertos in me; *this* is what I'm about!"

TP: One final question, Glenn. If a record store flew off the planet into space, and our music was picked up by alien creatures who knew nothing of the circumstances of its composition, or what the pieces were meant to represent, or what the composer's reputation was, what pieces would be taken to heart by this alien community? In this context-free situation, what would make their top ten?

GG: [laughs] Once again, I don't know quite how to answer that! But I will say that one composer who wouldn't make it – except for the last pieces and a few of the first ones – is Beethoven. He is one composer whose reputation is based entirely on gossip. The "Grosse Fuge" would make it, the early piano sonatas, maybe the Op. 18 quartets, but I don't think that there is room in space for the Fifth Symphony. Not at all.